Sustainability has become a strategic impera[...] [...]tions remain unsure about where to start, h[...] be affected. Such an approach is doomed.

Fortunately, in this highly accessible guide Joanne Flinn provides a comprehensive road map for board members and senior management, detailing what they must consider and where they must lead.

Every board member should have a copy; every chair should build governance discussions around it; and it should be required reading for every director and every CEO.

Philip Forrest
Member of the Governing Council Singapore Institute of Directors

At last, a how-to manual on sustainability that prepares company directors for converting today's voluntary disclosures to tomorrow's preconditions for corporate survival. This easy-to-comprehend reference source, with its infographics, explanatory tables, and checklists, allows directors to become proactive champions for a healthier planet, whilst leading their companies to long-term, sustainable profits."

Kris Wadia
Board Director and CEO, Humanized Leadership

As organizational leaders and boards become increasingly aware of the complexity of the sustainability agenda, they can feel overwhelmed. This is where Joanne's book is essential. A simple but not simplistic, practical guide for organizational directors and leaders to understand the foundational role sustainability (people, planet, and profit) plays in governance. For leaders who want to ensure they are approaching and embedding this into the essence of their responsibilities and the fabric of good governance, this book is a must-read!

Rebecca Hill
Chair, auticon UK Advisory Board

Greensight gives leaders insights on how to turn good intentions into impactful action. With the magnitude of challenge every board faces, this easy-to-read book distills the essences of change management and contextual foresight into an actionable handbook for directors and other leaders.

The urgency of the challenge and Joanne's elegant clarity for simplified action will help you start now. Do not await perfection or universal accounting regulations, thus wasting time we don't have while the planet burns. It is better start now with *Greensight* and learn from doing our best.

Martin Thomas
Co-author of The MultiCapital Scorecard,
former CFO, Unilever

This great book deciphers the complexity of the inevitability of sustainability. It is perceptive, well researched, and cogently argued. The alphabet soup within ESG has never been clearer. A straightforward, intelligent road map to mitigate existential risks!

A must-read for boards, the C-Suite, and management.

Tom Preststulen
Chairman, Elkem a.s.

Sustainability will be the single biggest trend shaping our future on the planet in the decade ahead. We must look at it as an opportunity to transform our approach to economics as we transition from the current linear systems and adopt circular approaches. *Greensight* provides an effective framework to guide this transition into a new way of thinking, where ESG is an integral risk and growth framework to adopt for organizations. Immensely readable and outlines a practical approach

Yash Mishra
Head Sustainable Investments, Taurus Family Office

Greensight cuts through the noise, providing a clear and concise guide for business, public sector, and civil society leaders to manage their massive local and global responsibilities. In each chapter, Joanne Flinn's experience as a coach shines through, providing an empowering set of principles and tools to address climate change and equity, our generation's greatest challenges.

Lauren N. Sorkin
Executive Director, Resilient Cities Network,
pioneered by the Rockefeller Foundation

In *Greensight – The Sustainability Guide for Company Directors*, Joanne Flinn provides a great reference for boards starting on their journey, or looking for structure in their sustainability road map.

While this book is suitable for mid-sized and large corporate boards, there is plenty that a small company board or entrepreneur can apply.

Note: this book is not a step-by-step guide for managing the media after a sustainability catastrophe! Instead, we are provided with succinct guidance to create a culture and structure a plan that will **reduce the risk** of such events.

The book highlights early on that, while sustainability may be a tool to set oneself apart, sustainability will, in the long term, be business as usual. This is a critical concept to fully appreciate. It is one that is likely, in time, to be forced on slow movers by way of tariffs, legislation, and taxes.

Much of the book is devoted to the considerations necessary for a board developing the business plan for a sustainable future, with extended analysis around stakeholder management and the roles of various C-suite members.

While covering core topics such as scope 1, 2, and 3 emissions, it also touches briefly on wider topics such as plastics and biodiversity. Perhaps most importantly, *Greensight* takes time to consider the implications for cost of capital and profitability.

Marrying the need to meet shareholder expectations and to satisfy a range of stakeholders has always been challenging, but today under ever-increasing public scrutiny, company boards have to stay ahead of the game.

It is rare in business that an industry follower or laggard can overnight become a leader, without some revolutionary development. Right here and now, there is the opportunity to be the green leader for a given industry, to innovate in a sustainable way. Joanne Flinn provides a road map we would all do well to at least consider.

Richard Hayler, FIoD FCA FCIArb CA(SG) CAIA CIA
Group CFO, Nutrition Technologies Member, Standards
Review Board, International Valuation Standards Council

As an investment lead, a strategic advisor, and a board director, I have worked for over two decades to enable investment and delivery of sustainable, resilient, and inclusive infrastructure and services across Asia and the world.

As the pace of change and volatility has accelerated, board directors and company leaders are putting more and more thought and resources into strategically future proofing our companies and their investment programs. In fact, to stay at the forefront in terms of risk management, regulatory compliance, market considerations, and even reputation, companies both big and small are also realizing that it is no longer optional but essential to put sustainability planning and action into the central part of our board agenda.

However, a key stumbling block is a lack of internal expertise to make sense of the mesh of regulations, criteria, and frameworks that have mushroomed in recent years. Even for investment and sustainability professionals, the rapid evolution of ESG nomenclature and proliferation of standards in recent years has it made it difficult to keep up and report against them to the various ratings providers.

Reading Joanne Flinn's new book *Greensight* reminded me just why she's so good. The book is a timely and authoritative synthesis of all the latest tools, frameworks, and action points on ESG, told in well-packaged and actionable bites. At the same time, Joanne writes in a fun and user-friendly style peppered with examples from her own extensive experience as a strategy consultant and a board chair. She looks at how things have evolved, but also peers round the bend to give a glimpse of what is likely to come.

There are checklists of useful framing questions that you, as a board director or CEO/CXO, can ask of yourselves and your team to get up to speed very quickly. And since she has taken care to offer frameworks and diagrams that are MECE (mutually exclusive and collectively exhaustive), this book is both a primer to get you started and a reference book you will dip into again and again. Boards and management would do well to buy *Greensight* and hand it out to their executives!

Supriya Sen
Senior Advisor at Mckinsey, NID Institutional investor in renewable and climate-friendly infrastructure

This timely, well-structured book addresses something I have seen first-hand—that boards (like many people) have their "general" understanding of ESG and their own biases around what they think that means for business. *Greensight* takes one on a useful journey of learning what the actual state of play is, what sustainability means, and how one ought to be approaching it—especially as a director. I recommend and advise all directors and prospective directors to read this book to understand this important issue. Frankly all senior managers in companies ought to read it, too!

Bill Bryant
Managing Director, Stolt-Nielsen, MEA & APAC

Greensight is a book for the times, as the broad theme of sustainability refashions business behavior and actions for stakeholders and guardians of governance. What is great about the book, is Joanne's clear sighted exposition of sustainability and where we are now, leading into how the environment and business behavior is evolving with clear thoughts on focused action. This book is a must read for today's business leader.

Rahul Gupta
Senior Fellow, Harvard University and Research Affiliate, The Lakshmi Mittal and Family South Asia Institute, Harvard University

If you want to get your business partners, suppliers, and network aligned with your sustainability efforts, give them *Greensight*. This way not only you but your entire supply chain will know what to do to stay on procurement lists, get referrals, and be future fit.

Nick Jonsson
Co-founder, EGN Singapore & Indonesia

GREENSIGHT

ALSO BY JOANNE FLINN

The Success Healthcheck for IT Projects
An Insider's Guide to IT Investment and Business Change

Calm
How to Stay Calm and Productive Through Crisis

EDITOR & CO-AUTHOR

New Eyes
The Human Side of Change Leadership

Unleash Your Voice
Powerful Public Speaking for Every Woman

GREENSIGHT

The Sustainability Guide for Company Directors

JOANNE FLINN,
MSID, MSc, BEc. Llb

*An invitation . . . to courage over fear,
joy over apathy, and to leadership that
creates value for today and our future*

To John and Alice

*For your many gifts to me, including life, creativity
and the knowing that we can do the needful.*

CONTENTS

FOREWORD

by Rafael Ramirez

This well-written, accessible book is positioned as a conversation between one board member (the author) and another board member (the reader). Joanne Flinn compellingly suggests the reader *should* be having this conversation—urgently.

The book is an invitation for board members to hold more courageous conversations with each other, as well as with the C-suite executives who run the company they govern.

The scenarios for putting this conversation off are increasingly untenable.

For the reader who is a C-suite executive, it is time to stop kicking the ball into the long grass, to act *now* before the costs involved in not acting or delaying jeopardize the survival of the business itself.

The author's incitement to more urgently and courageously address climate issue(s) is an attractive proposition, not least because inaction will indeed lead to incurring higher costs. And as she so cogently argues, further delay does not decrease costs, it guarantees their increase.

Doing the right thing for the climate is a director's fiduciary duty; not doing it means the company, and perhaps its directors themselves, might get sued—as Shell was, and found guilty in 2021.

I have served on four boards (and serve in one at the time of this writing). I have experienced first-hand how difficult it is for those of us who "get" the climate challenge to communicate its urgency and importance to fellow board members. This is particularly the case for those who are—rightly—focused on cashflow, reaching value generation metrics, and more generally securing or strengthening financial sustainability.

I was asked to write this foreword because I have argued[1] that the two concerns—financial and climate—cannot and should not be separated from each other, into separate departments focusing on strategy and sustainability.

As Oxford's first Professor of Practice, I have had the pleasure, over the years, of seeing many practitioner alumnae develop into what my late friend and colleague Donald Schön called "reflective practitioners." Reflective practitioners like Joanne Flinn stop and reflect (sometimes by writing a book) in a way that supports and furthers the work of other practitioners.

In these pages, Joanne Flinn reflects on her career as a board member and as an advisor. She highlights the current primordial importance to board members and C-Suite executives: it is still possible to do something about climate change.

---

1   Rafael Ramirez, *How to Get Corporate Strategy to Engage with Climate Change*, Knowledge at Warton, Nov 15, 2019, https://knowledge.wharton.upenn.edu/article/corporate-strategy-engage-climate-change/.

But the window of opportunity to do something meaningful and that actually works is closing. Choosing to continue harming future generations of people and destroying the biodiversity of animals and plants, the author argues, needlessly increases avoidable liabilities for individuals and for companies.

As long as company senior managers and supervisory board members elect to defer facing up to the damages that their companies are causing to the environment, this book will remain not only timely, but qualifies as an urgent read. With clear, forward-thinking guidelines for boards and every C-suite position, it is a call to act, now—before it is too late.

Rafael Ramirez
Board Member and Professor of Practice,
University of Oxford

THE DIRECTORS' CHALLENGE

Picture this: 20 deep-seated chairs, low lighting, wood paneling. When I first walked into the boardroom, I recognized the implications of my surroundings. This business was designed to last.

Not only was I on the board—at 22 and still studying law and economics, I was a named individual. Senator Michael Field of Tasmania had sent me a letter congratulating me for this appointment.

I discovered the business was steeped in unfunded debt. And that we would be severely challenged to pay that debt if it was called due.

Looking out the windows in that wood paneled room, up at the forests on the mountain behind us, I was struck by the core message of sustainability. As much as what I'd do as a director was about the financials, I had a responsibility to make sure the business would be around for the future. And that what we did would positively affect the environment around me.

At times, I've cursed and blessed that law degree, which gave me knowledge. In this situation, I knew I had potential civil and criminal liability. I could be exposed to charges of negligence and a failure to deliver on my fiduciary duty of care.

Some of our stakeholders were unimpressed with our choices when we restructured services, price points and expectations. And others were delighted.

That first board taught me that the court of public opinion was as powerful as the court of law and the exchequer.

Thirty years on, as we face the climate crisis, digitalization, robotics, and social change—sustainability for business leaders distills into three qualities:

- Sustainability of cash through value generation
- Sustainability of legacy through service to stakeholders
- Sustainability of planet through what we do to it and what it does to our business.

The inevitability of sustainability

Sustainability looks set to disrupt and change business every bit as radically as the digital revolution. It represents a transformational tsunami that is real, that is right now, and that will directly affect you and your organization. It affects your business model, your stakeholders, and your responsibilities as a director.

Every organization, in every sector, should by now be aware of this issue. Some, both large and small, have already taken first steps towards understanding, assessing, and responding. For boards and senior executives, the imperatives of a sustainability strategy should be a top priority.

One of the key challenges is that the nature of sustainability means that its impact extends beyond the traditional remit of organizations and into the broader areas of value chain and ecosystems. Which in turn threatens the foundational tenets of traditional management theory.

Greensight shines a light on the sustainability trend that increasingly affects director responsibility.

The issues of sustainability—governance, regulations, expectations, etc.—are evolving with each month that passes. Which means what was best practice only last quarter may now be standard practices of next quarter.

Greensight highlights strategic principles of sustainability for business so that you can focus on the significant elements while your teams focus on tactics and the very real on-the-ground challenges.

And you as a board member must navigate an increasing mountain of reports, standards, and consulting views about sustainability requirements, much of it couched in environmental language. It's like attempting to read Thai script when you only know the Latin alphabet. There is a dearth of simple, clear, easy-to-understand business literature on the subject. What's missing for you is the handbook outlining what sustainability means to you and how to approach implementing it for your business.

Greensight offers that level of guidance for you and for your team. This book is designed to help you evolve your organization to meet these constantly changing, all-encompassing challenges and seek out the opportunities that come with them.

Meet your guide

I grew up in the first Green Revolution. My father was a scientist. His work as an agricultural economist took me to Africa and Asia as a child. He'd bring rigorous science out to farmers, to make sure that science improved their lives and incomes. I swam in the waters of sustainability—on a globalized level—from day one.

After that initial board experience, I went on to run my first $10-million business at 23 and then sat on a $60-million board. Later in my career I became country head of PricewaterhouseCooper's financial services consulting practice in Thailand and then I sat on the IT Exco of DBS, an Asian bank. I've lived and breathed finance my entire professional life.

My professional focus is business transformation from a systems thinking perspective. You could say I'm a chip off the old block. Like my father, I believe we have what it takes to solve the world's biggest problems. I believe that business can be a force for good. I also believe it is in the best place to tackle what more and more individuals, companies, industries, and governments recognize as an existential crisis—climate change.

■ ■ ■

I certainly don't have all the answers. Over the last 30 years in my role as a director myself, as well as a strategic advisor, trainer, and coach, I've had the unique opportunity to see what really works in business.

I'm in the wonderful position where I get to have private conversations with top leaders in global companies and hear from them their struggles, dreams, and ideas. I also see what's getting in the way of them and their organizations. What they say to me in the secure confidential space of a coaching environment is quite different to what they say when they sit around the board table setting strategy or even what they say when they face other stakeholders and the world.

On the other side of the equation, when I run master classes for their teams, I hear complaints about how sustainability feels disconnected and not aligned to company culture. I hear when they feel held back and struggle with taking action.

It's from these observations, conversations, and independent research that the Greensight framework has emerged to help business leaders like you take on climate, sustainability, and transition.

Is this book for you?

I wrote this book for board members, chairpersons, CEOs, and C-suite leaders with responsibility for and accountability to deliver long-term value and align their organization to deliver strategy and sustainability.

This book is also for managers and any leader wanting to get an edge on sustainability and influence their organization's trajectory.

Greensight is particularly attuned to the needs of Chief Sustainability Officers (CSOs), who are increasingly charged with transforming the sustainability profiles of their organization and the organizations they partner with.

Navigating this book

Greensight simplifies the nuances of sustainability, firmly anchoring it into the world of business and distilling 10,000 pages of what can feel like business-speak eco-babble into 164 pages of actionable insights for executives and boards.

I'm not trying to detract from the scientists, environmentalists, and sustainability experts who have worked incredibly hard for 50 years—their field generates jargon, just like the worlds of business and finance do. This primer cuts to the chase for business leaders to focus on three key questions that will enable you to consider where your business model may be affected by sustainability.

Part One is the Sustainability Primer for Boards. This primer simplifies the alphabet soup of sustainability language, looks at two scenarios we face as leaders, helps you evaluate what (un) sustainability is doing to create or erode enterprise value, and takes you gently into the world of ESG (more formally known as Environment, Social, and Governance). We'll take a good look at stranded assets, a pressing danger facing businesses today. Then we'll walk through the 1-2-3s of sustainability that paradoxically help align stakeholder interests. Finally, we cover the six categories of sustainability impact.

In April 2022, the Intergovernmental Panel on Climate Change (IPCC) 6th report[2] said, "The evidence is clear: the time for action is now. We have to halve emissions by 2030." This is a huge challenge. And they continue, "We have options in all sectors to at least halve emissions by 2030." There is hope.

All things considered, the pressure on business to respond, act and even drive sustainability is accelerating. I call this pressure the Sustainability Surge.

Part Two focuses on capital and stakeholders. *Greensight* examines sustainability through the lenses of capital, shareholders, and stakeholders. Business exists to solve problems and serve. Stakeholders drive external pressure to act.

Recent research[3] reveals a surprisingly wide range of organizational readiness and progress. Some organizations admit to having barely awoken to the challenges ahead. Others have embarked on profound transformation while often acknowledging that they are still barely scratching the surface.

From this research, four sustainability responsiveness typologies emerged, embodying four models of strategic response to the Sustainability Surge.

The sustainability responsiveness typologies can help you benchmark your business, align your people, and take action. This allows you to reduce risk while growing your business.

2 *Climate Change 2022: Mitigation of Climate Change.* Contribution of Working Group III to the Sixth Assessment Report of the Intergovernmental Panel on Climate Change, April 2022.
3 Flinn, J., Wilson, A., *The Imperative of Sustainability Responsiveness*, May 2022.

Part Three looks to action. Sustainability is not about being a bystander, it is about what we do in business. Like staying healthy, sustainability is active.

The final section of *Greensight* outlines the sustainability governance action framework you can put in place as a board, as board committees, and as C-suite executives to respond to the imperatives of sustainability. When I facilitate sustainability strategy workshops with leadership teams, this framework gives them a strawman to adapt to their own unique situation. I share it so that you can act more swiftly.

There are three criteria that hold the keys to unlocking transformational levers and accelerating sustainability:

(a) *leadership agenda*
(b) *ambitions of assessment of ESG factors: Environment, Social, and Governance*
(c) *ambition of responses to Pledge, Plan, and Progress (the 3Ps of Sustainability)*

Business response lags behind

Our findings in *The Imperative of Sustainability Responsiveness* report showed that businesses were not fully embracing the urgency or the importance of sustainability. As of Q1, 2022,

- Just 27% of respondents said sustainability was a critical item embedded in their strategy and sector;
- 30% of respondents were waking up to the importance of the issue to their sector and business;

- The remainder (43%) reported that sustainability was either dormant or newly emerging as a key factor.

Future impact on specific business models will define the ambition of transformation required.

Ignore sustainability imperatives at your financial peril

The Sustainable Accounting Standards Board's (SASB) Climate Risk 2021 edition reviewed 77 industry sectors, focusing on industry-specific risks and opportunities that are most relevant to returns and **long-term enterprise value**. SASB found that all 77 sectors are affected by climate change, either through impact on balance sheet assets and liabilities or through profit and loss statements, revenue, and costs.

These risks may impact customer interest in your products and services, the viability of suppliers and price points, and technology options available, as well as generating stranded or toxic assets and contingent liabilities.

In addition, banks and financiers are increasingly expecting sustainability insights based on Environment, Social, and Governance (ESG) reporting as part of their credit assessment. Stock exchange listing rules from the Singapore Stock Exchange (SGX) to the New York Stock Exchange (SEC) are implementing disclosure requirements for transparency.

Over a coffee with me, Su-Yen Wong, Chair of the Singapore Institute of Directors, made it clear that simply ticking the boxes and playing the rankings game is greenwashing. In her view, it's the board's job to get buy-in on sustainability from everyone else involved. She provided three framing questions boards and leaders can ask themselves:

- Are we doing what's right?
- Do we have the right attitudes and culture in place?
- Are we moving forward knowing nothing is perfect?

While sustainability is complex any way you look at it, it can be simplified and it is actionable. *Greensight* is your board guide for sustainability action.

Your next step

The effects of sustainability requirements in the business world are becoming apparent at lightning speed, and this puts significant pressures on boards to stay current.

To stay ahead of the curve, with updates arriving in your inbox, and access to diagnostics and checklists, join **GreensightGuide. com**.

And now, let's get into the alphabet soup that is sustainability so that you are well positioned to make the decisions you need to as a director and leader.

PART 1

THE SUSTAINABILITY PRIMER FOR BOARDS

Simplifying the alphabet soup

As climate change and sustainability notch their way up the enterprise agenda, it's easy to get lost in the acronyms—and then to push it all aside as something for later or for someone else.

However, in my conversations with global CEOs, all of them report that sustainability is a KPI set by their boards and that this sustainability KPI is between 25% to 50% of their annual targets as CEOs. They also tell me that their teams don't "get" the alphabet soup that is sustainability.

What follows in this section is a primer to help you, your teams, and your results. I'll show you how to add a 4% margin to your profitability, how to save 2% on your cost of funds—and how to stay out of jail.

Business risk, impact, and opportunities

Sustainability has layers

There are three layers to sustainability for business. Each has a different focus, yet all three align toward the same purpose. As a CXO or director, you need to answer these three questions:

1. What is climate change doing to your business, and you to it?
2. How does this create or erode enterprise value?
3. What are you disclosing in your financial and statutory statements?

Miss one out and your business may not be sustainable, which could leave you facing bad PR or even fiscal penalties.

What is climate change doing to you, and you to it?

Let's look at sustainability in the big picture of climate and humans on the planet. Climate change raises a two-sided question. What impact does it have on the sustainability of your business (revenue, customers, supplies, risks)? And what impact does your business have on climate and thus the broader sustainability of our society and environment?

When customers, regulators, and investors ask, "What is your commitment?" they have their eye on two major scenarios for the future.

The two scenarios

Let's simplify them in business terms:

The Rusty Red Scenario.[4] Are your business and your investment practices aligned to a future that will see global temperatures rise by 3°C or more? This is the dire world of the planet burning and social collapse. Ratings agency Standard & Poor's reports that 66% of companies are unknowingly operating this way, even those that have publicly committed to "going green."

The Green Scenario. Are your business and your investment practices aligned to a future that sees a global rise in temperature of 1.5°C or less? This is the climate that has so far allowed human beings to flourish—and it's the sustainable scenario that CEOs are increasingly being tasked to commit to.

The Rusty Red Scenario

The rusty red scenario has two sub-futures: dire and diabolical.

Dire is when our enterprise and business systems adjust to simply enduring a +3°C world. Hundreds of millions of people are displaced, food systems are stretched, and what were once classified as 100-year floods, fires, and droughts are happening every 20 years or so. Dire is not good.

---

4   This scenario is as destructive as rust. We call it *rusty* rather than just the obvious *red* because in Asia, red is a colour of prosperity and the 3°C+ world is not prosperous for Asia. More people risk loss of livelihoods and homes in Asia in the rusty red scenario than anywhere else in the world.

Diabolical is dire on steroids, with 100-year disasters every decade. This is the trajectory of current business practices, which lead to a potential +5°C world.

Think about it like this. Our current business lifestyle means we've gotten more than just a bit overweight and out of shape. The doctors have pointed out that diabetes and cardiac arrest are imminent. Step 1 is to stop adding the gunk into our system and Step 2 is to clean up what we've already done to ourselves.

To achieve the green scenario, we must play a different game.

The Green Scenario

Our green goal is to stop adding carbon to the atmosphere and then to remove what's already there in excess to promote a return to a climate that's healthy for humans and other species—and, at the same time, to create highly valuable businesses and a thriving society. *#Healthy&Wealthy*

In a business health paradigm, the green scenario has three sub-types:

- **Going net zero:** this is where a business offsets their carbon footprint without curbing current carbon input. It's the binge and exercise option.
- **Going true zero:** this is where a business shifts how it operates so that it's using processes and products that do not create carbon. This is the option to maintain your weight and reduce health risks.
- **Going regenerative:** this is where a business decides to get healthier and fitter than ever before. It's getting carbon-neutral and dropping those kilos. It's a distinct lifestyle change.

Clever thinkers step ahead

The prescient among us are already looking at three additional elements.

Are your planning and processes creating a *just* transition? This asks you to look at the social impact of your strategy and how you can make it socially fair for the disadvantaged.

Are you aligned to science-based targets? Such targets look across the economic system that businesses align to so that we don't inadvertently do damage somewhere else while we take action in any one dimension.

Are you simply addressing your own internal operations or are you looking at what it really takes to create value? (Expect much more on this topic when we discuss green ambitions spanning Scopes 1, 2, and 3 in a later section of this primer.)

Investors, regulators, and customers are asking for insight on sustainability and your climate risks. They look at how well you've refreshed your strategy to incorporate your climate goals. They'll ask about your climate ambition—what scope you are committing to and what you are doing to achieve it.

It's the business version of keeping up good relationships, not over-training, and making sure your ecology is sustainable.

Committing to the green scenario has direct economic value *now*. The EU is introducing a 4% levy on goods that are not produced in alignment with the EU taxonomy on sustainability. They are doing this to create a level playing field so that imported goods pay an equivalent price to the cost of carbon in the EU. This carbon border levy is called the Carbon Border Adjustment Mechanism (CBAM).

If you are an Asian business with end customers located in Europe, this will increasingly affect your profit.

What gets measured

On the basis that what gets measured gets done, there are a variety of initiatives to assist you in adapting to the green scenario.

There are policy initiatives. The EU's New Green Deal is the driver behind CBAM. The Sustainable Development Goals (SDGs) are a set of 17 goals with 156 sub-elements that, while primarily designed for countries, can also provide insights for companies assessing where they have positive or negative impact.

There are measurement initiatives. The Global Reporting Initiative (GRI) helps you understand and report impact across a range of issues such as climate change, human rights, and corruption. *MultiCapital Scorecard*, a book and free, open-source management tool by Martin P. Thomas and Mark W. McElroy, provides a practical effective business reporting road map.

There are also investor initiatives. The Principles for Responsible Investment (PRI) is the future-facing investment paradigm where money is expected to do more than simply make money—it's expected to create an impact, too. Issue-focused initiatives are increasingly active; for example, Climate Action 100+ ensures that 100 of the world's largest corporate greenhouse gas emitters take necessary action on climate change.

Science says we have under a decade to get green. And then another decade to get greener so that we head off the worst of the rusty scenario. This is where the *by 2030, by 2040*, and *by 2050* markers come into the discussion.

Your climate ambition

In a nutshell, your **climate ambition** is your commitment to:

(a) achieve net zero, true zero, or regenerative status,
(b) your scope of ambition (1, 2 or 3, see page 39), and
(c) your timeline for each element (by 2025, 2030, 2040, etc.).

Your **climate strategy** is your plan to respond to external changes while delivering on this commitment—along with your financial and other commitments.

In the absence of a stated climate ambition or strategy, any enterprise continuing to conduct business as usual (BAU) is defaulting to a rusty scenario pathway.[5]

Standard & Poor's reports that major global companies in their S&P Global 1200 index are on track for +3°C warming, falling 72% short of required emissions reduction to achieve the Paris Agreement.

If your enterprise does not know its sustainability status, there may be unknown, unquantified liabilities in the not-too-distant future—rendering your business unsustainable to stakeholders and the planet.

In the next section, we focus on what sustainability does to create enterprise value—and what unsustainability, or BAU, does to erode it.

5   https://www.spglobal.com/esg/education/essential-sustainability/climate/transition-risks. Accessed 5 May 2022.

What does [un]sustainability do to create or erode enterprise value?

How to save 2% on your cost of funds

This question is forward-looking, scenario-based, and pathway-dependent. In other words, it is independent of which of the two futures you are acting towards—the rusty at +3°C or the green at under +1.5°C.

For those wondering about the middle ground, there is none! If you're not actively working towards a global temperature increase of 1.5°C or less, you are, by default, in the rusty zone.

> *For those wondering about the middle ground, there is none! If you're not actively working towards a global temperature increase of under 1.5°C, you are, by default, in the rusty zone.*

This step in the transition strategy is where boards, investors, insurers, and financiers are asking for insight, transparency, and disclosure of your climate risks, strategy, and ambition.

The rusty scenario has transition costs. So does the green scenario. They each come with risks, opportunities, and implications to enterprise value.

As a board or C-suite, use your enterprise climate strategy and ambition to signal a commitment to deliver.

If you've yet to set your climate ambition—as outlined above: your commitment to (a) net zero, true zero, or regenerative, (b) your scope of ambition, and (c) your timeline—there is no better time to do so.

Now, as a senior executive team, you need to work through the risks and implications of rusty and green for your business model. There are significant opportunities in the green scenario if you know how to look for them.

This is not simply an internal discussion on targets and metrics, risk management, governance, and strategy.

Aiming is not acting

Given that 64% of enterprises say they are aiming for green with publicly disclosed carbon targets yet are acting in line with the rusty red scenario,[6] there is currently a gap between stated strategy and executed strategic actions—a gap that is becoming more publicly visible daily as disclosure requirements move from voluntary to mandatory.

This gap is increasingly of interest to regulators and investors.

Financial system regulators, including central banks like the Monetary Authority of Singapore (MAS), call the rusty scenario an existential treat. They want to see commitment to action resulting in a green scenario from banks, asset managers, insurance organizations, and other members of their financial ecosystem.

Climate-related business disclosures are being required by several agencies, including:

6   https://www.spglobal.com/esg/education/essential-sustainability/climate/transition-risks. Accessed 5 May 2022.

- The Financial Stability Board (FSB), who are responsible for global financial stability
- The Sustainable Accounting Standards Board (SASB) who have spearheaded the development of climate reporting, standards
- The International Financial Reporting Standards Foundation (IFRS) who lead the financial reporting standards globally

Investors, insurers, and financiers are looking for accountability

Investors are looking for disclosures too. BlackRock, CALPERS, and other institutional investors are looking for transparency. More and more, investors' view of their fiduciary responsibility extends past making sure they get their capital back in addition to targeted returns. They realize that an ROI based on the rusty scenario has a poor overall return.

Insurers want to know if you are insurable. Does your business have assets that might be at risk? Investors and financiers want to know if you have assets that might lose significant value (become stranded) or even have negative value (become toxic). Standard & Poor's analytics suggest that all major business have at least one significant asset in the latter category.

What insurers, investors, and financiers are after when they ask you to report is disclosure and transparency on your climate ambition, and proof that what is being said is being done. You don't want to be accused of "greenwashing" on social media or anywhere else.

As a collective, the finance, insurance, and investment industries are establishing new standards with shared methodologies. While some of these standards are recommended as good practice, several will be enforceable through regulation or industry bodies in the very near future. Why? These industries want to know that risk is priced correctly and that you are insurable.

In the next section of this primer, we focus business risks, impact, and opportunities in the much-mentioned ESG elements of the sustainability alphabet soup.

The next cup of alphabet soup: ESG

What are the ESGs?

The ESGs (Environmental, Social, and Governance) are a set of criteria that describe your practices across a broad range of elements.

These criteria began to be used in the 1960s as socially responsible investors excluded stocks or even entire industries from their portfolios based on their activities—like tobacco or firearms production or involvement in South Africa's apartheid regime. In 2004, as ESG investing matured, with data supporting the assumption that ESG factors have financial relevance, the UN Secretary General Kofi Annan invited over 50 CEOs of major financial institutions to a joint initiative to integrate ESG into the capital markets. This led to the *Who Cares Wins* report, which made the case that embedding environmental, social, and governance factors into capital markets creates better results for investors, the markets, and society. In parallel, the Freshfield's report shows that ESG issues concretely impact valuations. These made way for the launch of the Principles of Responsible Investment (PRI) and ESG as we know it today.

Today, EGS covers:

Environment – pollution, waste, and environmental impact

Social – modern slavery, diversity, and inclusion and payment conditions

Governance – decision-making, anti-corruption and bribery, risk management, and business codes of conduct.

Note: This list is ever evolving, as the list of elements within each of the ESGs continues to morph and expand. In The Imperative of Sustainability Responsiveness, *we surveyed Asian leaders to see the extent to which they'd engaged with these ESG elements. You can find survey results to benchmark yourself in Part 2.*

Pragmatically, each element speaks to a contingent business risk that affects reputation, cash flow, and market valuation.

Let's drill into the G part first, as it is the element with the least public visibility and conversely, the one with most actionable internal controls.

Businesses are currently designed as if climate change is not an issue. Yet the storms, floods, and fires we are experiencing along with scientific data from the Intergovernmental Panel on Climate Change (IPCC) indicate that we are firmly on the rusty pathway.

There will be costs to transitioning to survive in the rusty scenario. And yes, there are costs to transitioning to create the green scenario as well. To put it bluntly—rusty red or green, transition investments will be required.

Investments are a decision. Decisions have parameters, express or implied. These parameters are governance.

Investments and decision-making

For a leadership team, each decision made is either rusty or green. It's either consistent with your commitment or not. Your decisions are where governance shows up with a capital G.

> *To put it bluntly—rusty red or green, transition investments will be required.*

And that is where, in the medium to long term, enterprise value is either multiplied or destroyed.

Formal ESG reporting is gaining steam. What was the Non-Financial Reporting Directive (NFRD) has now become the Corporate Sustainability Reporting Directive (CSRD), applicable to listed companies in the EU, including SMEs and large companies. CSRD is coming into force from 2023 to 2026, based on organizational size.

As of January 1, 2022, the EU taxonomy on sustainable actions comes into effect. This defines green investment and supports the prudential soundness of green assets according to the European Banking Authority (EBA).

While the CSRD and EU taxonomy apply directly to the EU only, they will influence any business that trades with the EU or whose customers do. Those who trade directly will ask their suppliers to disclose their carbon impact to prove eligibility to avoid that 4% levy.

Those who trade *indirectly* with the EU will also be required to disclose their carbon impact to stay on procurement lists. Your downstream customers need this data for their own declarations.

Sustainability beyond carbon

Tackling two big sustainability issues more specifically are standards that address climate and nature—through the Taskforce for Climate-Related Financial Disclosures (TCFD), the Taskforce for Nature-Related Financial Disclosures (TNFD). These two standards address financial reporting of sustainability.

Natural systems issues like deforestation, loss of habitats, and species loss all have their impact on human quality of life and are intrinsically part of the interrelated challenges to sustainability. Other standards address reporting on physical sustainability impacts.

Both TCFD and TNDF are backed by the FSB and the SASB. G7 leaders recommended that the TCFD become a mandatory reporting requirement for business, so it is likely to happen soon.

With IFRS Foundation, SASB and the International Integrated Reporting Framework (short coded as <IR>) aligning to create a common standard, proactive action will reduce implementation pressure. It will also assist in staying on procurement lists run by business partners further along the sustainability responsiveness journey than your business.

What does this mean for enterprises like yours?

Going forward, governance requires transparency to investors. Investors are setting expectations through board resolutions, premiums, and costs of funds. Insurers are reevaluating insurable events and premiums.

In recent private conversations, CFOs of multi-billion-dollar organizations have confidentially shared that the cost of funds in their rusty scenario business areas is 4% higher than in their green scenario businesses.

The finance world is increasingly pricing in climate risk. Anticipate that disclosure practices will crystalize as the TCFD comes into more active force in the next two years.

Prepare for equivalent moves in the following areas in the near future:

- Impact on biodiversity and nature
- Use and protection of waters and marine resources
- Pollution prevention and control
- Social impact of supply chains
- Transitioning to a circular economy.

Being proactive in these categories leads to practical preparation and risk mitigation as a CXO, board member, or named individual.

What's in your financial and regulatory statements

One of my goals in writing this book is to help keep you out of court, both the court of public opinion (with consequent reputational damage) and the court of law—the one that leads to jail.

Legal opinion in Australia, Singapore, New Zealand, South Africa, USA, Canada, Malaysia, Hong Kong, Japan, India, and the UK makes it clear that directors and named individuals face civil and criminal responsibility for actions and inaction in where climate is concerned.

The Commonwealth Climate and Law Initiative (CCLI) and the Smith School of Enterprise and the Environment (SSEE) from the University of Oxford engaged senior general counsel (the cream of the legal fraternity) in each of these countries to assess director liability and climate change.

To quote the Singaporean opinion:

> *"Directors of companies are required under Singapore law to take into account climate-related risks in their decision-making process, failing which they will be liable for breaching the duty to act in good faith in the best interests of the company and the duty to exercise reasonable diligence."*[7]

This is more than ensuring your organization can make verifiable disclosures.

It's ensuring your strategic planning bakes sustainability in upfront. It's ensuring your finance organization shifts from a backwards view of accounting statements to a forward view of climate risk and scenarios.

It's strategic sustainability, not simply reporting.

---

7   *Directors' Liability and Climate Risk: White Paper on Singapore,* Dr. Ernest Lim, Associate Professor Faculty of Law, National University of Singapore, April 2021, p. 4. See also Jeffry W.T. Chan, S.C. Joseph Chun, Ernest Lim, Peter Doraisamy, Queck Wen Jian (Gerald), *Legal Opinion On Directors' Responsibilities and Climate Change Under Singapore Law,* April 2021.

ESG adherence is business opportunity

Practically speaking, it begins with getting your revenue team to realize going green is sustainable profit generation, not a pain-in-the-butt box to tick for compliance. And it's about the compliance and red-tape folk shifting from *here's why we can't* mode into *here's how we can*.

This means rapid shifts in fast-moving, uncertain environments.

This is about your business sustainability. This is about your ability to sign off your annual report to say that you are not trading while insolvent—and soon, not trading while unsustainable.

To do this, you must understand and clearly show that you've taken the necessary steps to address ALL the letters in the ESG alphabet soup.

> *This is about your ability to sign off your annual report to say that you are not trading while insolvent—and soon, not trading while unsustainable.*

And separately, your children and grandchildren might just thank you for saving their planet.

The dirty secret of stranded assets

As businesses begin to wake up to the dual challenges of sustainability and understand where a rusty or green transition would take them, they may discover that some of their assets are at risk of being stranded.

A stranded asset is a piece of equipment or a resource that once had value and produced income but no longer does so. Usually, this is the result of an external change like shifts in technology, the market, regulation, or social habits. An old-school example is how the introduction of electricity led to a drop in demand for whale oil, which led to a decrease in the need for whaling ships. Those assets literally ended up stranded on seashores. Modern examples include investment in Betamax or CD-ROMs. How many offices still have unused CD-ROMs floating around in some cupboard? These, too, are stranded assets.

While some would see this as a natural part of the competitive landscape of business, CFOs are concerned for their investors as these assets, if not yet fully depreciated, must then be written off on the company accounts, affecting the balance sheet.

At one level, one would hope that astute investors have priced this into their share purchases.

Now, some industries are heavily focused on stranded assets, and such a focus may lead to rusty red-transition thinking. Accepting a write-off is not easy. Industries like steel, which uses huge amounts of fossil fuels in the coke that fires its furnaces, must make tough choices to invest in developing new technologies, while at the same time they face writing off the major capital investment that makes a steel furnace. Taking this to an investor focused on present-day returns can generate pushback, adding to the mindset challenge for green transition thinking.

For you, here and now, there is an additional nuance to stranded assets that will help you reduce your risk.

Three types of assets

Back when I ran the Financial Services Consulting Practice at PricewaterhouseCoopers in Thailand, I lived first-hand through the impact of stranded assets. When the Asian Crisis hit and the economy tanked, banks began to collapse. Many of their assets were loans to companies and individuals who could not pay. As part of our process of restructuring the banking system (a topic for another day), we distinguished three sets of assets.

There were those that were still productive, and sadly there were fewer of these than we'd have liked.

Group two was those assets that were now stranded—for example, sugar mills that were now sitting idle, with demand for sugar way down, and that were essentially unsellable.

And then there was the third category, the kind you want to look out for and proactively manage: those assets that were not simply stranded, but now toxic and therefor far more dangerous. They had negative impacts on the value of the organization. You can get away with letting stranded assets sit and rot away, much like the wooden boats of yesteryear. But toxic assets put risk and liability on your books.

It's not simply that you won't get the price you'd like for what was once a productive asset, it's that the liabilities linked to these toxic assets can bring you down.

Note: you may have originally invested in those assets in good conscience, in full alignment to your fiduciary duty as a board member or executive. It's what's happened since that you need to stay on top of.

An example from the real estate sector:

> Asbestos was once embraced as a building material because it is a very effective fire retardant. It was later discovered that over time, breathing asbestos particles could lead to an irreversible condition called asbestosis, as well as lung cancer and death. As a result, many countries have banned it.
>
> Asbestos companies faced litigation for the health costs and for the cleanup costs of removing asbestos sheeting from buildings. This put significant contingent liability on the books of those businesses and destroyed many of them.
>
> In Australia where I come from, if you buy a building containing asbestos and you want to renovate it, you must get rid of the asbestos first—like cleaning up toxic assets to stabilize balance sheets, avoid further losses, and begin regrowing a business.

It's important that your risk appetite for stranded and toxic assets is clear to your executive team, as well as to your executive teams in subsidiary and associated entities.

The tragedy of the horizon

Recently, during a C-suite strategy refresh and long-range planning session I facilitated for a Fortune 100 business in Asia, it was clear that they wanted to do the right thing. Their goal was to add a billion to their top line in the next three years, but they'd not received a clear sustainability directive from their board.

This challenged the rigor of their long-range plan, as they could not incorporate sustainability goals appropriately into their

Capex requests and strategic plan. Between you and me, their first-cut plan was not sustainable for a net-zero world.

To be fair, as for many listed companies, their C-suite definition of long range was three years. Yet decisions and investments have longer-term consequences on the 5, 10, and 50-year horizons. This shortsightedness contributes to the risk of stranded assets.

Mark Carney, formerly head of the Bank of England, calls this mismatch in planning timelines the "tragedy of the horizons." He tightly ties this tragedy to climate change and financial stability. Capital markets, long-term investors, and rating agencies are increasingly asking for alignment of horizons.

While you are not a central banker, it's important to ensure, as a board, that your strategy has strategically sustainability over a longer term than three years. To play green, you need multi-decade horizons like 2030, 2040, and 2050.

Reducing the Capex risk

Here are two scenarios-based questions that will help your teams with Capex decisions:

- If within a decade, we are to live and breathe the green scenario, deliver on a net-zero commitment, and use offsets only as a last resort, what would need to change about our plan?
- If we continue as planned, operating under BAU or the rusty scenario, which assets would be stranded and at risk of write-off?

This will help your teams highlight any significant investment or asset where value creation is affected either by the rusty or the green scenario. These two questions may also surface as yet unexplored business opportunities in the green scenario.

Why care about toxic assets in the context of sustainability?

Directors are at risk of civil and criminal liability

In many cases, there are warnings of impending issues. With climate change, there have been warnings for decades now. When the man on the street knows about it, it's hard to say, as a director, that you don't.[8] This means that legally, there is a reasonable expectation for you to understand and act to mitigate those contingent risks. A chartered accountant would say these are "foreseeable contingent liabilities." Ouch.

Carbon and other greenhouse gases have accelerated climate change to the point where the legal system (through director responsibilities) and the financial system (through their fiduciary responsibilities on investors) will expect each business to own its contribution to the crisis.

Balance sheet degraded

A company's carbon footprint may move from being a contingent risk to become actual liability. And if this liability is more than

---

8   You could. You'd be setting yourself up to be accused of acting negligently. Now, since you are reading this book, I know you care, you are concerned, and you are interested in improving the sustainability of your business. The risk reduction that comes with taking action is a bonus.

your business can manage, it will be toxic. Balance sheets will be affected.

This is where proactively aiming for under +1.5°C and operating with a green mindset becomes a benefit. You'll be further along in the transition process and thus more sustainable as a business. You'll also have reduced your risk.

Extended liability for clean up

Here's a heads-up: the cleanup process associated with toxic assets can implicate more than the original companies involved in the creation of the toxic product. Broader parts of the supply chain can be pulled into accountability.

> For example, a party that buys a building and puts employees into it has a duty of care to the staff. In the case of asbestos, it's in their interest to clean that building up before putting staff into it. During the next decade the environmental equivalent of this duty of care will likely become part of our legal system, with cleanup accountability becoming the norm.

In IT, there is a concept called legacy risk, or more informally, a hangover. It's an acknowledgement of the cost of earlier short-cuts taken in design and decision-making. Those decisions were usually made to be expedient in service to short-term P&L.[9]

---

9   The cost of this to business is a 30% portfolio write-off and can be addressed by a mindset focused on long-term success. J.A. Flinn, *The Success Healthcheck for IT Projects* (Wiley 2010).

As the world changes and the extra costs and consequences of old decisions become apparent, that hangover must be addressed in the interests of long-term sustainability.

In many cases, that hangover is preventable through structured thinking. Aiming for under +1.5°C as a business through a net-zero ambition and by adopting a green mindset will help you reduce legacy risk.

The 1-2-3s of sustainability

For companies, boards, and the C-suite, the first business-oriented sustainability standard, the Greenhouse Gas Protocol (GHG Protocol), came out as a voluntary standard in 2001.[10] You can see it as the grandfather framework. GHG Protocol thinking defines the expectations we face today. Like a good broth, it has flavored the sustainability alphabet soup pot.

The GHG Protocol is designed to address the impact of business on the planet. It's not designed for our ease or convenience. It is designed to enable us to see, own, and act on externalized costs to the environment. It is green scenario thinking.

The principles underlying the GHG Protocol and its operationalization over the last 20 years show through in other protocols and

---

10 The GHG Protocol addresses six greenhouse gases. These are: carbon dioxide (CO_2), methane (CH_4), nitrous oxide (N_2O), hydrofluorocarbons (HFCs), perfluorocarbons (PFCs), sulfur hexafluoride (SF_6), and nitrogen trifluoride (NF_3). Carbon dioxide gets the most press as it's the largest by volume. Methane is 85 times more dangerous to global warming over a 20-year period.

conventions, so it's necessary to be aware of the implicit framework embedded in sustainability standards.[11]

For you, I've distilled pages of dense, dull, but important documents into 300 words of transferable principles and a couple of graphics!

What do you do and what is its impact? This covers both your legal entity and entities where you have direct control while taking into consideration those where you have influence through decision-making and operating policies (including joint ventures, franchises, and operating agreements). This is called Scope 1.

You and Your Controlled Entities

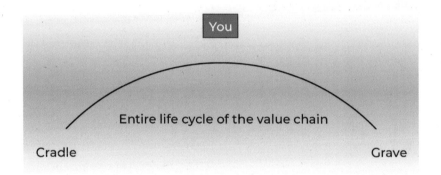

Figure 1 Scope 1

---

11 Standards including GHG Protocol and its two subprotocols, TDCF, TNCF, SBTi, GRI, PRI . . . the alphabet soup covered earlier. The Carbon Disclosure Project (CDP) builds on GRI and the GHG Protocol as a disclosure regime covering over $100 trillion in assets.

What resources are critical for your business and what is their impact? This covers key inputs. For example, few businesses generate energy, but energy is critical for operations. On this basis, carbon from energy production is part of what's called Scope 2.

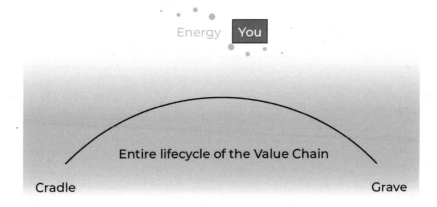

You and Your Controlled Entities

Energy Used

Figure 2 Scope 2

What do you need to prosper, and what impact does this have? This covers your value chain. If it helps you make a profit, you own it.[12] This applies both to your supply chain upstream and to your downstream distribution through to customers. This is called Scope 3.

12 GHG Protocol p. 20.

You and Your Value Chain
Energy and Waste

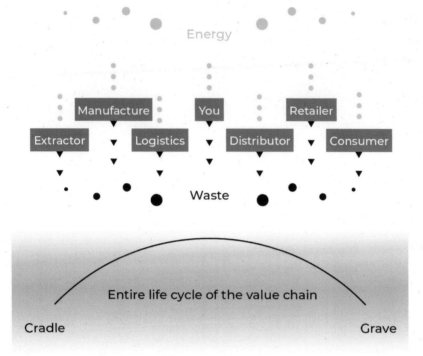

Figure 3 Scope 3

In the words of the Greenhouse Gas Protocol: "A company that derives an economic profit from a certain activity should take ownership for any GHG emissions generated by the activity." This applies to Scopes 1, 2, and 3.

This principle stretches our thinking and responsibility past the veil of incorporation.

Summarizing the Scopes:

Scope	Covers	Broad Principle
Scope 1	You, joint ventures, franchises, and operating agreements	You use it
Scope 2	For emissions: energy providers	You need it
Scope 3	Value chain upstream and down	Impact of products and services that enable your profit

Scope 3 encompasses strategic choices, investments, and asset creation.

For example, when IKEA first measured their greenhouse gas impact, they found that 66% of their greenhouse gas emissions were in Scope 3, from customers travelling to stores. As a result of this insight, store location policies were adjusted.

The implications of Scope 3.

The traditional boundaries of business responsibility, accountability, and liability are changing. With greenhouse gases, we can't handwash and say someone else did it simply because it was a different business that produced the pollution.

This is distinctly different to rusty scenario processes where businesses could use separate legal entities to outsource, reduce, and manage risks and liabilities. Passing the buck is a central tenet of BAU.

The designers of the GHG Protocol, along with the authors of newer protocols and standards, focus on the overall outputs of the value chain. This is what affects climate. These protocols encourage us in business to look from end to end and ask: are greenhouse gases going up or going down?

The upside of Scopes 1, 2, and 3 is that when you and your value chain work out how to reduce any part of your impact in any scope, you benefit. And so does the planet.

Increasing transparency and long-term thinking

The goal of protocols and standards like the GHG Protocol, TCFD, TNFD, SBTi, GRI, and PRI is to increase transparency and long-term thinking. Transparency enables measurement. Measurement aids accountability. Accountability drives ownership. Ownership drives action. What gets measured gets done.

The structure of these standards is designed to help us as leaders, as boards, and as C-suite teams. While some of it can feel like enviro-techno babble, the data generated helps us link our externalized impact to what we do in business.

This makes it easier to see impact for stakeholders right now, in a few years, and in the longer terms of 10, 20, and 50 years out. This makes the tough challenges of trade-offs between stakeholders clearer and reduces the potential for stranded assets.

For boards, the standards assist in risk reduction, aligning with the long-term viability of the business, and creating insights to assist in decision-making and strategic directions-setting.

Are service businesses at risk?

Services and digital sectors are exposed to climate-regulatory risks.

For a **digital company**, this includes hardware like data centers and electronics as well as software services, be they web- or cloud-based. For a soap manufacturer, this covers washing and drying as well as heating the water to do the washing. For any company with a physical product or a service that uses physical products, this includes end-of-life treatment like waste recycling, landfill, and incineration.

For a **financial services company**, this picks up the externalities associated with how your clients make a profit. The ESG reporting expectations of banks, asset managers, insurers, financial advisory services, and the capital markets are in part driven by their need to report Scope 3.

Professional services like auditing, design, marketing, media, and taxes may be overlooking Scope 3 implications for now, but like financial services firms, they should anticipate responsibility and exposure. These industries also need evaluate their client portfolio for Scope 3 implications to avoid exposure.

If you are a digital or services company, your value chain uses real-world assets and energy. Your value chain footprint counts.

The bottom line: Scope 1, 2, and 3 reporting is about what is actually being emitted.

Remember, removals and reductions are accounted for separately. The goal is aggregate changes in global emissions.

The power of common language

The standards also mean you have a common language, set of metrics, and basis for alignment across your value chain.[13]

Disclosure implies sharing information within your value chain: with business partners and with the public, including investors, banks, and communities. Listed entities and B corporations will see increasing expectations for substance in their sustainability reporting. Private companies will see expectations from banks and clients, both of whom will need insight into operations for their own Scope 3 disclosures. All businesses will see increased transparency expectation from customers and employees.

While you may not legally be required to disclose Scopes 1, 2, and 3, the shift in expectations from other parts of the value chain may nonetheless require these disclosures for you to continue doing business with them.

If your value chain includes a big player with a Scope 3 goal, they'll be looking for your pledge of ambition and updates on your progress.

> For example, in Singapore, many banks are asking their service providers, including consultants, designers, and IT for their sustainability commitments. These commitments are needed to stay on procurement lists.

Anticipate that in the very near future, banks that are asking today for your pledge will also ask for transparency of progress. They'll need it for their own 1-2-3s.

---

13   The EU Taxonomy released in 2020 is the de-jure reference point for business.

It's all about value

As your organization becomes increasingly familiar with the 1-2-3s, your tone from the top will count. You set the culture and norms for the decisions and data we see. There are five norms to be aware of as you look into your value chain:

- Substance: it's not about form, it's about what's really happening
- Completeness: it's about **all** impact
- Consistency: for comparability and accountable progress over time
- Credibility: with sufficient accuracy for you and others to make decisions
- Clarity: presentation is factual, neutral, and understandable.

Measure it ALL in the 1-2-3s

The 1-2-3s are about data. You don't know what you don't know until you measure.

Do an assessment so that you have data. Until your company gets hard data through a robust assessment of your actual impact, it's not possible to make an informed decision about what's material.

Materiality is used to set a threshold of what needs attention.

> For example, in the finance world of business, you might say that if something represents under 2% of revenue, it's not material.

> In the physical world of climate, with Scopes 1, 2, and 3, you need to measure actual physical world impact, not financial

impact. In the GHG Protocol case, you are measuring carbon, methane, and other gases.

Think about it as looking to see where you have trace elements in your production process. Back in the day, fancy top hats made in the USA and Europe used a minute amount of mercury-nitrate to felt the hat. Then it was realized mercury made hatters mad (now you know where the expression "mad as a hatter" comes from). Paint, particularly white paint, used to contain lead, and children's toys with lead paint poisoned children, who inevitably put toys in their mouths—resulting in brain damage. Trace elements can create outsized impacts.

In practice, a small activity from an accounting perspective may represent a big impact from a carbon perspective.

For example, in 1996, United Technologies baselined their jet fuel usage in product testing, thinking it was insignificant. On the financial side it was not seen as material. In that world it could be excluded from reporting. When they measured actual impact on the physical world side of things, they discovered the jet fuel usage was between 9–13% of their total annual energy usage and thus their carbon footprint.[14]

Because of the trace element effect, the GHG Protocol says assess **all** your processes, not just the big ones or the financially important ones. Assessments give you data about your physical impact.

---

14 *Greenhouse Gas Protocol*, by World Resources Institute and World Business Council for Sustainable Development, March 2004, p. 44.

Valuing your value chain

The point of Scope 3 is to create an incentive for collaboration between multiple entities so that emissions and other negative externalities are reduced across society.

While the five norms of substance, completeness, consistency, credibility, and clarity focus on **all** your process and the impact they have for good reason. The standards setters were well aware that we humans have biases and a tendency to ignore what seems small. Understanding climate change means dealing with many trace element situations, where a small activity can create big impacts.

In practice, an effective starting point is to focus on major activities and work out where major impacts are (remember those trace elements). Yes, it is possible to reduce disclosure and justify an exclusion. However, an exclusion is a bit like an audit qualification—admissible but best avoided.

Sustainability redefines director responsibility and liability

Between Scope 3 reporting required by stakeholders in your value chain, reporting needs for listed companies, and the general counsel view that directors face civil and criminal responsibility in respect of their actions toward sustainability—director responsibilities and liabilities have shifted.

And they will increasingly see greater shifts.

In Singapore, directors of listed companies must go through mandatory training on their environmental responsibilities.

Beyond Climate

In this section, we'll cover the collective tipping point of action, as well as frameworks and standards that are already affecting some businesses and are likely to affect many more in the near future.

While carbon and climate are getting the headlines, recognize that sustainability is about more than emissions. There are other parts of sustainability that are hitting and will hit board agendas in the very near future.

Over the last 50 years, scientists and activists have worked with governments and countries to recognize how our current industrial system affects the sustainability of human life on the planet. In November 2022, we saw a sea change in business awareness and acknowledgement of the issues at COP26 held in Glasgow.

If you are not familiar with COPs[15] and other climate treaties, it's not that you were missing out over the years. Many of the treaties targeted specific issues and were not mainstream business. They do, however provide the basis of thinking and thus accountability for what we now think of as sustainability.

The pace at which a COP pursues its goals may be set by multi-country negotiating blocks, political positioning back home, and on occasion, high-stakes holdouts. Unlike a board meeting comprising 6–15 people, such meetings involve hundreds of

15 When the UN wants to move a topic forward, they create a Counsel of Parties (a COP), which meets as frequently as needed to achieve a set goal—often a treaty. You'll see there are COPs for climate, for nature, and for waste.

countries. While a COP may be convened in an attractive location, participants may not have time to see much of the local beauty! The real negotiations can happen late into the wee hours of the final days.

On the planet

In 1992, the Rio Earth Summit established 27 principles for sustainable development. Yes, these have been around for decades! For those of us in business, the key principles are as follows (paraphrasing the extensive UN documentation for your ease):

> **The principles** recognize a state's sovereign right to exploit its own resources in accordance with its own policies, without harming the environment elsewhere (Principle 2); the right to development (Principle 3); environmental protection as an integral part of development (Principle 4); sustainable development that requires reducing "unsustainable patterns of production and consumption," and that promotes "appropriate demographic policies" (Principle 8); access to information and citizen participation (Principle 10); the precautionary principle (Principle 15); and the polluter-pays principle, including the internalization of costs and the use of economic instruments (Principle 16).

> In their words: Principle 15 (the precautionary principle) of the 1992 Rio Declaration states that "where there are threats of serious or irreversible damage, lack of full scientific certainty **shall not be** used as a reason for postponing cost-effective measures to prevent environmental degradation."

For businesses, these principles distill down to the idea that it's fine to exploit resources— as long as you don't harm others. Pollution is considered harm to others.

> **On the climate:** the convention initially intended to limit emissions of carbon dioxide—at present the largest contributor to human-induced changes in radiative forcing—to 1990 levels by 2000. It stated the very strong objective: "stabilization of greenhouse-gas concentrations in the atmosphere at a level that would prevent dangerous anthropogenic interference with the climate system . . . within a time frame sufficient to allow ecosystems to adapt naturally."[16]

> The Rio Convention established a financial assistance mechanism to support its implementation in developing countries.

> Part and parcel of the climate process established in 1992 was and remains financial assistance to those who need it to recover from damage created by climate change, to accelerate adaption to the and to enable equivalent quality of life as the developed world enjoy.

In other words, the summit proposed stabilizing the climate and financially assisting any actors who need it. This can be seen as a cost internalization of the polluter-pays principle.

Things progressed over the next 40 years. Rio's intentions moved forward with the Kyoto Protocols in 1997, which saw a shift to commit to reducing greenhouse gas emissions. This was

---

16 FN 3 in RIO Summit doc 3. UN Framework Convention on Climate Change, 9 May 1992, article 2.

operationalized in 2001 with the GHG Protocol, which businesses can commit to on a voluntary basis. The Paris Agreement (COP21) in 2016 set out to substantially reduce global greenhouse gas emissions in an effort to reduce global temperature increase in this century.

In 2021, António Guterres, the UN Secretary General with the IPCC scientific reports, recognized the climate situation as Code Red. Staying with the rusty scenario was too dangerous.

This accelerated the Race to Zero movement. The Race to Zero includes 1,049 cities, 67 regions, 5,235 businesses, 441 of the world's biggest investors, and 1,039 higher education institutions. These "real economy" actors join 120 countries in the largest ever alliance committed to achieving net zero carbon emissions, by 2050 at the latest. Collectively, these actors now cover nearly 25% of global CO_2 emissions and over 50% of GDP.[17]

This collective has the joint commitment to act to transition to a low carbon economy consistent with a temperature increase that stays under +1.5°C compared to the pre-industrial period.

Guterres's Code Red and the Race to Zero drives the business goals of net zero, true zero, and regenerative emissions.

The Glasgow Climate Pact of November 2021 aims to turn the 2020s into a decade of climate action. It includes strengthened efforts to build resilience to climate change, to curb greenhouse gas emissions, and to provide the necessary financing for both.

17 https://unfccc.int/climate-action/race-to-zero-campaign accessed 18 April 2022.

The polluter pays

In the rusty scenario, it is fine to pollute if there are no rules preventing it. Costs are externalized. In the green scenario, true costs of production, including pollution, are now recognized. It's like how the game of rugby recognized that neck tackles lead to players being hurt and, in some cases, becoming paraplegics. The International Rugby Federation revised the rules of the game: no neck tackles. Since this went into effect, we see a higher standard of play.

The green scenario is also a higher standard of play.

EU's carbon border adjustment mechanism (CBAM) and other carbon pricing mechanisms, including those set by the Taskforce for Climate related Finance Disclosures (TCFD), reflect these principles.

Countries are taking action.

It's clear where all this is headed in Singapore. The government and the central bank, the Monetary Authority of Singapore, both refer to climate change as an existential risk. This is strong language coming from a very formal and conservative set of leaders. Singapore's target is to reach net-zero emissions by or around mid-century. Some have challenged the government that the country had not committed to act fast enough. Having lived in Singapore for some years, I know they only make statements they know they can deliver on. So, when recently they updated their target to say by mid-century, it was clear they'd found a credible pathway to this goal.

In their March 2022 budget, the government of Singapore announced that the cost of carbon will increase a minimum of tenfold over the next decades from its current S$5/tCO2e (5 Singapore dollars is approximately USD$4), set in 2019 and covering 80% of total carbon emissions. This is well below Sweden's USD$135/tCO2e and Switzerland's USD$100/tCO2e. In 2024, in Singapore it will increase to USD$18/tCO2e and in 2026 it will increase to USD$32/tCO2e, with a view to reaching USD$36–58/tCO2e by 2030 (SGD $50–$80). This will have auxiliary price implications across the Singaporean business ecosystem.

For boards, there will be shifts like this not only in Singapore but worldwide. Carbon price is a resource cost. And look at what Singapore has announced as a pathway—where could you find opportunities for your business or value chain?

On plants and animals

Again, I'm paraphrasing the extensive UN documentation for your ease of reading:

On biodiversity. The 1992 Nairobi Conference established a treaty with three goals: the conservation and sustainable use of biological diversity, and the fair sharing of products made from gene-stocks. Governments were expected to develop plans for protecting habitat and species; provide funds and technology to help developing countries provide protection; ensure commercial access to biological resources for development and share revenues fairly among source countries and developers; and establish safety regulations and accept liability for risks associated with biotechnology development.

Financing of action to address impact is factored in.

A series of COPs has progressed this important topic. Some of the better-known ones include COP12 in Lima in 2014, COP15 in Kunming China in 2021, and COP16 in Turkey in 2022.

Anticipate the announcement of a binding framework that applies to counties in 2022. Like what we've seen in carbon, there a Taskforce for Nature-Related Finance Disclosures (TNFD).

> **On forests.** The need for a treaty was recognized with 17 non-binding principles. These apply to all forests, from the tropical to the temperate.
>
> Forests are recognized for their capacity to slow climate change. During the Glasgow Climate COP26, world leaders from companies and countries pledged to end deforestation by 2030.

The astute reader will notice that the treaties and agreements COPs produce apply to governments and not to businesses. However, the Glasgow COP26 signaled a joint alignment for public entities (governments and countries) and private ones (industries and businesses) on the broader climate agenda.

On plastic waste

Plastics are an extremely convenient product. They were revolutionary back in 1862 when first discovered, and since then they've given humankind manufacturing capabilities unconstrained by the limits of nature. For example, elephants no longer needed to be killed for ivory to make billiard balls, since plastic would do instead.

Fast-forward to today, when the total amount of plastics produced thus far is now greater than the combined weight of all land and marine animals alive today.[18] Yet, only 9% has ever been recycled. It turns out that while the recycling symbol means it can be recycled, it doesn't mean it will be.

In practice, plastic is designed to be used once, after which it ends up in landfills or dumps, is burnt and becomes atmospheric pollution, or ends up in waterways and oceans. Microplastics (defined as pieces less than 5mm in length) are so pervasive that we humans consume about 5 grams of the stuff, or the same size as a credit card, each week.[19]

March 2, 2022, a UN gavel banged when 175 nations agreed to begin writing a treaty on plastic waste. Here's an extract (so you can enjoy the distinct flavor of UN language):

> "1. *Requests* the Executive Director to convene an intergovernmental negotiating committee, commencing its work during the second half of 2022, with the ambition of completing its work by the end of 2024;
>
> 2. *Acknowledges* that some legal obligations arising out of a new international legally binding instrument will require capacity building and technical and financial assistance in order to be effectively implemented by developing countries and countries with economies in transition;

---

18 Elhacham, E., Ben-Uri, L., Grozovski, J. *et al.* "Global human-made mass exceeds all living biomass." *Nature* 588, 442–444 (2020). https://doi.org/10.1038/s41586-020-3010-5.

19 WWF with University of Newcastle, Australia Research, by Kala Senathirajah and Thava Palanisami, "How Much Microplastics Are We Ingesting?: Estimation of the Mass of Microplastics Ingested," 11 June 2019 news release.

3. *Decides* that the intergovernmental negotiating committee is to develop an international legally binding instrument on plastic pollution, including in the marine environment . . . which could include both binding and voluntary approaches, based on a comprehensive approach that addresses the full lifecycle of plastic."

Notice the expected pace of change embedded in this agreement. Instead of 30 years to implementation, the timeframe is 2 years. This agreement spans plastic waste on land and in the water. It also addresses the full plastics life cycle.

This last point is a heads-up regarding the increasing shift towards a circular economy where businesses will be expected to design products and services not only to potentially be recyclable, but to ensure that they are both recyclable and *recycled*.

Clever thinkers look ahead

Circularity is coming. Smart money is looking at this for business model design. The post-waste value chain is a circle where energy is green and waste is redesigned out, recycled, or reprocessed.

Anticipate a Taskforce for Plastic Waste-Related Financial Disclosures in the near future.

Business coalitions and think tanks ranging from the Alliance to End Plastic Waste (AEPW) to the Ellen McArthur Foundation and the Minderoo Foundation are actively engaged in plastics-based circularity. AEPW is a $1.5-billion fund with a specific charter to eliminate plastic waste. Their ambition is to do this by 2050.

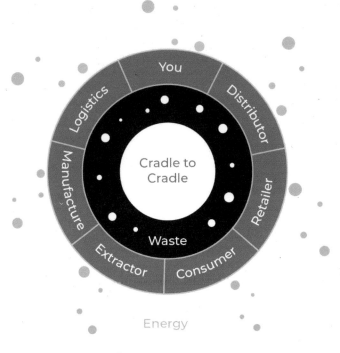

Figure 4 Circularity

On community

While there is significant and much-needed focus on business impact on the planet through carbon, greenhouse gases, biodiversity, water, pollution, and waste, this in no way reduces the equivalently significant action underway on the social elements of ESG.

Business leaders who have walked ahead on this journey say they wish they'd paid more attention to S elements earlier.

Like the E element of ESG we discussed above, there are increasing regulatory pressures underway through global standards that affect market access. The EU Mandatory Human Rights and Environment Due Diligence Framework, released in draft form in February 2022, is two to three years away from implementation and enforcement. The Australian Border Force is already enforcing modern slavery directives for trade and supply chains crossing into Australia.

Reputational risks can be significant in this area. Witness the reputational damage that the Blackwater massacre had on the US Military reputation; that the exploitation of migrant workers had on FIFA, the men's soccer World Cup, and Qatar; and that Tesco's modern slavery had in their Malaysia and Thailand business.

What counts

Climate and carbon are firmly on the agenda. Management consultancy McKinsey & Co. recognizes momentum has shifted, acknowledging "net-zero commitments are the norm."[20] This shift gives businesses a new organizing principle.

The fact is carbon emissions and climate change are an increasing visible part of the Sustainability Surge. In the business world, the definition and scope of understanding of sustainability is being refined and matured.

This is not something we need to do on our own in business. We can leverage the EU Taxonomy on the Sustainable Economy. It

20 Harry Bowcott, Daniel Pacthod, and Dickon Pinner, "COP26 made net zero a core principle for business," McKinsey Sustainability, Nov. 2021.

provides a common language and a clear definition of what business can consider as a sustainability action.[21] This gives you a checklist to align to.

If you operate or trade into the EU, you'll be affected by these criteria already through the EU's Corporate Sustainability Reporting Directive (CSRD). The CSRD applies to large companies (over 500 people) and to companies that are listed as of October 2022. This directive is expected to progressively apply to smaller organizations. EU companies need to report on sustainability– and they need to report Scope 3. This means businesses in Asia trading with Europe will be affected.

With 940,000 companies listed on Bursa Malaysia, the Malaysian Stock Exchange, Datuk Muhamad Umar Swift–the CEO of the exchange–asks pointedly of businesses in Malaysia, "Is your profit sustainable?" With the carbon border adjustment mechanism (CBAM) coming into operations in Europe, Malaysian businesses supplying that market will be affected. If information is not verifiable and not embedded in the way business is done, Malaysian businesses will lose market share.[22] In his view, sustainable profit creates long-term attractiveness for investors.

International business has a short window in which to prepare. The EU has designated 2023–2025 as a period for data collection and disclosures without financial obligations, enabling

21 The EU Taxonomy is science based so that fluffy actions that look good without substance are not credited as sustainable. The fact that it's science based helps you know your business value chain is aligning to a common definition and measurement– which is useful should your business want to set Scope 3 pledges.

22 Datuk Muhamad Umar Swift, CEO of Bursa Malaysia, speaking at the Cooler Earth Summit, 2021.

third-country producers and importers to prepare for the obligations arising in 2026.

What will be counted on the sustainability agenda?

First and foremost, businesses will be looked at to be environmentally sustainable.

At the most fundamental level, this comprises:

- Doing no significant harm. In other words, do good in one place while not doing harm elsewhere.
- Compliance with minimum social safeguards to secure human well-being without harming the environment or human and non-human lives.
- Compliance with technical screening criteria, such as scientifically validated methods like the Sciences Based Targets initiative (SBTi).

Corporate governance standards in Singapore[23] and the EU[24] expect boards to have a sustainability strategy that addresses human rights and environmental due diligence. Anticipate that the S element of ESG will increasingly be integrated into disclosure requirements, rating, and market research.

23 *Code of Corporate Governance* (2018) issued by the Monetary Authority of Singapore. https://www.mas.gov.sg/-/media/MAS/Regulations-and-Financial-Stability/Regulatory-and-Supervisory-Framework/Corporate-Governance-of-Listed-Companies/Code-of-Corporate-Governance-6-Aug-2018.pdf
24 See the EU Directorate General of Justice and Consumers, the EU Mandatory Human Rights Due Diligence Framework.

Six categories of sustainability impact

Leaning on the EU Taxonomy, here is a handy heads-up for priority of focus. It is helpful to see these as six categories where your business impacts and is impacted by sustainability:

1. Climate change (mitigation and adaption)
2. Sustainable use of water and marine resources
3. Protection and restoration of biodiversity and ecosystems
4. Pollution and waste prevention and control
5. Communities and well-being
6. Transitioning to a circular economy

In practice, see these six categories as a system where each effects the others.

While four of these categories are about planetary stewardship, failure to address the fifth, which is about people, can have significant implications for your license to operate. Item six is a heads-up to a shift toward a model of capitalism founded on stakeholder interests, not simply shareholder primacy.

Under-actioned

Many businesses are yet to step into action. In a recent pulse survey of 100 executives in Asia, *The Imperative of Sustainability Responsiveness*[25] reports that few were addressing all the current elements that comprise ESG.

25 Flinn, J., Wilson, A. *The Imperative of Sustainability Responsiveness.* 2022

Environment

While the materiality/relevance of each environmental factor may vary based on sector, eight environmental factors are yet to be widely built into sustainability response, as the chart below shows.

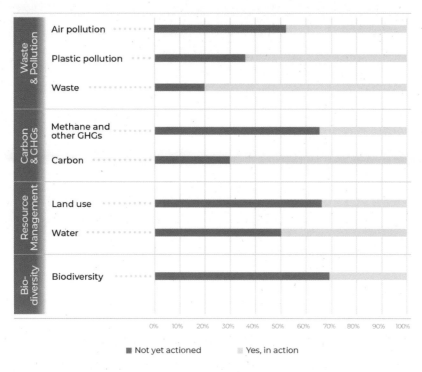

Figure 5 Unactioned environmental levers

The dark bar represents business leaders reporting that they have not yet addressed these elements of environmental sustainability. The light bar highlights those who have.

Businesses that have yet to address these elements may face unanticipated risks to medium-term license to operate and funding challenges, in addition to finding their access to talent more difficult.

Social

Comparatively speaking, environment has received more attention than the social elements of the ESGs. This shows in the degree to which organizations have engaged with the seven social-based levers of change we see in the table below—four at the operational level and three addressing organizational structure.

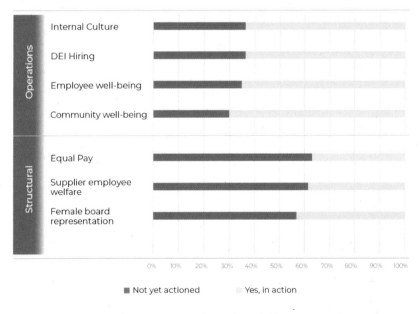

Figure 6 Unactioned social levers

The dark bar represents business leaders reporting that they have not yet addressed these elements of environmental sustainability. The light bar highlights those who have.

Most leaders have already engaged one or two of these operational levers, showing a commitment to progress. However, a significant minority are leaving some critical levers unaddressed. With the attention investors, customers, and employees place on social elements, if they're left unaddressed, a business will most likely slow down or eventually find success threatened.

ESG reporting, investors, media, and NGOs are placing considerable attention is on equitable structural change. Given how prominently these issues are playing in the press, it's surprising that these levers are being under-utilized. Those organizations that have yet to address these issues are facing significant risk, potential backlash, and lost opportunities.

Governance

Governance is directly within leadership and organizational control. There are eight governance-based levers of change—four at the operational level, two at the structural level, and two addressing license to operate.

Most leaders have engaged one or two operational levers, showing a commitment to progress.

However, a significant minority are leaving some critical levers unaddressed, which will most likely slow down or even threaten eventual success.

To stay in business, problem-solving and value creation are essential.

Critically, few organizations have tightly linked sustainability to the fundamentals of business cash flow.

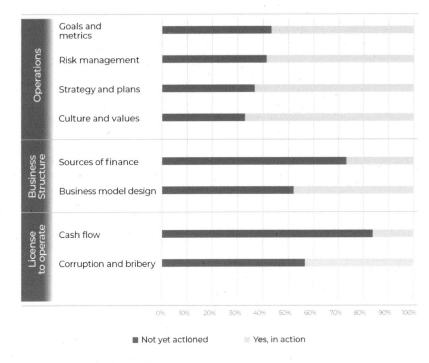

Figure 7 Unactioned governance levers

The dark bar represents business leaders reporting that they have not yet addressed these elements of environmental sustainability. The light bar highlights those who have.

Some organizations add a second E and even a third E to ESG, making it EEESG, to factor in economics and ethics. However, business governance includes attention to financial outcomes, just like it includes leadership style, fiduciary responsibility, and adhering to regulations and the law.

Leaders whose organizations struggle with taking action on sustainability may find that tightening links between ES and G through the business model helps address the inaction gap. For example, when a decision is made, have formal delegations of authority (DLA) for impact to the environment or social elements that are acceptable as well as a DLA for financial spending.

> For example: Consider how an ESG DLA may have reduced the risks to the board and chairman of Rio Tinto in the case of the destruction of Juukan Gorge. Rio blew up the 46,000-year-old sacred site and rock art at Juukan Gorge to extract $135m worth of iron ore. This led to the chairman's resignation, a parliamentary inquiry, and a court order for full restitution and rebuilding of that site.

Business model implications

As a board, evaluate your business's strategic fitness over the 5- to 10-year horizon and then the 20-year horizon to ensure that you are fit for the future. This means tracking to where the future will be, not aiming to be where the others were last year.

Look for second-order implications. Not just to your direct business per Scope 1, nor simply to your key inputs per Scope 2, but to your value chain per Scope 3.

Work this through in a structured process. There are many moving parts, between your commercial goals, the 1-2-3s in your value chain, and the ESG elements. Do this at the same time as you enact changes in your stakeholder needs, technology trends, and other business scenarios. Keep in mind the unfortunate possibilities of inflation, war, famine, and pestilence. Keep in mind the possibility of successful positive outcomes, too!

As a board, identify the broad parameters you need to see in the operational strategy. As a C-suite, work through the implications of these moving parts. When I have lunch with the chairman and CEOs after a Greensight workshop, they often tell me the workshop discussions, while not always comfortable, improve the rigor of their strategy, helping them to respond faster and more effectively when the next challenge to their strategy arrives. That these workshops improve the defendability of their decisions is a bonus.

The factors that businesses are expected to address will expand beyond the eight environmental, seven social, and eight governance factors covered here.

Given the lead time it takes to address many of these elements, proactive planning, action, and business transformation are required not only to deal with the very real implications of climate transition but also the very real implications of transparency in each of these ESG elements. Your responses may shift from isolated and operational to structural and strategic, in order to integrate and align action within your own organization and, increasingly, with other organizations.

There will be increasing push for certification and assurance to show that your business has assessed sustainability responsiveness and is acting on those findings.

Business model readiness for sustainability

Stress-test your business model for risks, breaking points, and the potential for new value creation. Where could you find opportunities for your business or value chain?

You may find it helpful to identify where your business model (or lines of business) sits on a scale. This lets you evaluate how ready you are to respond to the imperative of sustainability.

1	2	3	4
Your assessment finds no need to change anything due to sustainability pressures.	Your assessment finds a small need to change due to sustainability pressures. All can be delivered within current (2–3 year) timelines.	Your assessment finds some need to change due to sustainability pressures. Some changes will take longer than current (2–3 year) timelines.	Your assessment finds substantial need to change due to sustainability pressures and opportunities. Implementing some changes will take longer than current (2–3 year) timelines.

Sustainability Responsiveness Impact Scale

This assists you in future casting and evaluating the forward-looking statements you make in published sustainability reports.

Boards will be signing off on sustainability reports across all aspects of ESG, not simply the ones that are easy to address. Executive teams will be looking to address ESG issues more comprehensively.

In Singapore, sustainability reporting is already required of all listed entities. As of December 31, 2021, directors sign off on sustainability statements with the same legal responsibility as for financial statements.

We'll see companies engage in assessment standards that will be more urgent and more radical. Those that wait are at increased risk of disruption, regulation, and irrelevance.

The bottom line

- While carbon-focused, climate-related action has been well underway for decades now, sustainability action related to biodiversity and forests is picking up pace. Likewise, anticipate increased attention on the social elements of ESG.
- Anticipate action on plastic waste, water, and marine resources.
- Carbon pricing as a mechanism is maturing and hitting the top and bottom line.
- The user-pays principle is well established and will increasingly be looked to as a source of accountability.
- Sustainability transition financing needs will increasingly be on the national agenda. This will flow to the business agenda.
- Businesses need to:

  - ☐ Stress-test their strategies and business model for sustainability to move past carbon to looking at their impact on biodiversity, water, and waste
  - ☐ Expand sustainability strategies past the E of environment to include the S of social
  - ☐ Shift from a compliance mindset to the green mindset where sustainability is a business value driver.

PART 2

CAPITAL AND SUSTAINABILITY

In Part One, I distilled the vast complexity of sustainability into a practical primer for executives. This primer covered the three major components of sustainability. It began with the three critical questions you need to ask as a board.

1. What is sustainability doing to you?
2. What are you doing to sustainability?
3. What are you going to do about (1) and (2)?

We simmered the alphabet soup of sustainability down into a digestible broth. Then we covered the principles of Scopes 1, 2, and 3 and the implications these have on board responsibilities. And then we delved into the ESGs (Environment, Social, and Governance), looking closely at the elements that make up E, S, and G. I gave you benchmarks so that you can identify where your business sits in respect of actions taken. The section wrapped up with a look at the implications of sustainability for various business models.

In this section, we focus on capital and stakeholder alignment.

As directors, we know that the law does not see ignorance as an excuse. In the UK, Australia, Hong Kong, Singapore, South Africa and Malaysia, the general counsels who wrote the advisory briefs are not a standard bunch of silks. They all see sustainability as being mainstream enough for us to be accountable for it. If, like many directors, you are new to grappling with sustainability and responsibility, don't panic. The point of these 1-2-3s is to get you up to speed on established principles so that you don't get caught out—personally or professionally.

Why you want to read this right now: a sea change is underway for businesses and their boards. Enterprise and executive responsibilities are changing, and the rate of change is in constant acceleration. Change always presents opportunities. But it's important to know what we are responsible for and how to recognize those opportunities, as contexts change.

Long term

As directors and executives, we know our responsibilities are about the long-term success of the company. Yet in terms of sustainability, we've got several time frames to address.

Let's look at some of these terms from the perspective of money—in other words, from the point of view of investors, shareholders, bond holders, and other sources of funds like creditors and options holders.

While all these entities are concerned with money, their interests and time frames vary. As leadership, parsing up these stakeholders gives insight into the game each is playing. This stakeholder awareness helps in deciding which form of money you need to pay attention to on the sustainability front.

The interests of capital providers vary significantly

Keep it simple, as your capital structures will vary significantly. Each of these sources of money and capital have different interests in sustainability:

- Movement traders: they are investing in your story for the moment. They might not care at all about your sustainability since long term for them may be no more than 30 minutes.
- Creditors: you must pay them as and when your contract says you will (or else you'll be trading while insolvent). They'll care about your sustainability position based on their value-chain concerns.
- Banks: time frames will depend on the loan type, ranging from at-call to decades. Category 15 of the GHG Protocol includes investments and ESG reporting requirements mean that banks increasingly expect you to disclose your sustainability position as part of your fundraising. They need to roll up your position into their book.

- Private equity: investments may be held in portfolios for 5–10 years. While this may imply you don't need to consider a 20-year horizon, the value of the investment and its cash-out value in a decade will be influenced by your sustainability position. It will affect the multiples you are able to gain.
- Pension funds and sovereign wealth funds (SWF): this is big, long-term money. Blackrock and Temasek Holdings (a Singapore SWF) are both clear that a planet that is healthy in 10, 20, or 50 years is in the best interests of their investors. They are looking for sustainability with substance.
- Family offices: multi-generational wealth frequently takes a very long-term perspective (20–60 years), although they will consider short-term opportunities.

Look at your reporting horizon along with the visibility you have into the interests of your financial stakeholders. The interests of financial stakeholders exert pressure that creates trade-offs between long-term sustainability and immediate profit. It is a tension that boards need to manage.

During Paul Polman's time as CEO of Unilever, he was very clear to his investors that his time frames were long term and sustainability focused. He told shareholders who wanted only short-term returns to go elsewhere. And he looked for investors with similar investment values and time horizons.

Sustainability investment reaches the tipping point

The increasing availability of impact financing and green financing makes it easier to find funding that is aligned to sustainability-based investments. (In early 2022, $84 trillion of funds under management are captured by net-zero goals[26]; this is up significantly from 2% of a few years ago.[27])

Even a few years ago, only a few specialist investors who cared personally about sustainability wanted substance in sustainability actions. The number of investors interested in sustainability has tipped from a few innovators into an early majority. As a board and leadership team, you should presume that 50% of your funding sources care about sustainability if you source them from the capital markets. This figure is likely to shift substantially in 2022 and in 2023 as the Bank of International Settlements (BIS)—the central banker to central banks—and the IFRS Foundation announce mandatory practices that will affect banking and finance systems as well as corporate reporting.

Climate does not comply with the Rule of 72

At a practical level, it pays to understand the pace of change—in particular, whether it's accelerating. Here is some perspective from a family office CFO who was kind enough to share his analytical lens with me.

Sustainability means dealing with a situation that does not comply with the Rule of 72.

26 https://www.cib.barclays/our-insights/10-esg-themes-for-2022.html.
27 'Investing for Impact: The Global Impact Investing Market 2020,' International Finance Corporation, Jul 2021.

The Rule of 72

In finance, the Rule of 72 states that if something increases by 1% every "period," it will increase by 100%, or double, over 72 periods. The global economy, for example, grows at 3–3.5% per annum. It's a gentle compounding.

Doubling in a shortening series

The impacts to our planetary ecosystem are creating economic costs that are doubling in a series that is getting shorter and shorter. What took 25 years then took 18, then 12, then 9, 6, and 4 … The actual financial costs are doubling in fewer and few years. So even if governments don't act (and one hopes they do, so that the playing field is leveled), costs that were once externalized are increasing now internalized.

This is visible in the significantly greater cost of wood and the significantly cheaper cost of renewable energy these days.

The economics of acting and investing for sustainability will make better and better sense each year, and wise investors will invest early in sustainability for better long-term capital preservation (Rule 1 of long-term wealth is, don't lose money; Rule 2 is that it is a probability game).

Early action is in your favor

Early action allows time to work in your favor by giving you and your business longer to understand what's going on. It's not a one- or two-year play to defer till later. Do things now so that you can learn under less pressure.

In the venture capital world, just like in business, it takes three to five years for a new business, startup, or service to come to fruition. Starting your sustainability refit now gives you a longer runway to address the inevitable zigs and zags you'll end up taking as you operationalize new realities.

Watch out for default thinking

As leaders, take note. The Rule of 72 is default thinking. It implies a gradually accumulating change, a context in which there is not often a significant cost of delay. Pushing something out to deal with it in five years under the Rule of 72 will only mean 6.5% cost increase. This looks like a 1.5% cost penalty per year of delay—apparently easy for a future board or management team to address.

Climate change does not conform to the Rule of 72.

When doubling time on a series gets short, as we are seeing in terms of climate change, a five-year delay in action is not 1.5% increase in the cost of action—it may be a 100% increase in the cost of action! It could be substantially more if the series should double on a two-year cycle.

Climate economics is reshaping entire industries

Investment plays that actively move toward a world where temperature increase is kept under +1.5°C will redefine the economic climate in ways that both increase learning and mitigate risk for you.

For whom does your business exist?

"I care about environmental sustainability. But I'm owned by an oligarch," an executive said to me over coffee in 2021. Oligarchs and other shareholders with a financial extractive focus have not necessarily bought into the shift happening in stakeholder capitalism. For investors who are solely financially focused, regulation and public exposure is simply a cost of doing business. For others, stakeholders are a vital way of doing business.

It's about stakeholders

As a board, be clear where you sit on this spectrum.

Shareholder primacy

At one end of the spectrum, there are businesses where shareholder primacy and maximizing profit are the only bottom line, and for whom sustainability means accepting that civil and criminal liability may occur.

Listed companies trying to maintain this position will be challenged by transparency and sustainability reporting requirements.

Sustainability is acceptable if it does not impact returns

Some businesses are more middle-of-the-road, looking at sustainability as a trend that need not damage returns.

Fund owners like Aberdeen see their net-zero targets and the move to low-carbon portfolios as something that will not necessarily cause a drop in performance.

Businesses that invest in sustainability as a reactive measure will be less likely to have their eyes open for sustainability-based opportunities.

Sustainability is stakeholder driven

On the other end of the spectrum are companies like Microsoft, Interface, and Patagonia that see themselves as stakeholder driven. The Lutheran Pension Fund see themselves as stewards of assets and accept that stakeholders expect them to rise to the sustainability challenge. For such companies, divestment is simply shuffling deck chairs (on the Titanic) when the focus needs to be on decarbonizing our business operations and entire value chains.

Where are your stakeholders driving you?

As a board, be clear where your business is playing.

- Is your financial focus on the short term or the long term?
- Is this focus stakeholder-centered short-term or stakeholder-centered long-term?

Your stance will influence your sustainability strategy and your growth strategy.

Your stance will also influence the tactics you use to reduce, offset, or divest on the carbon and waste front.

The green scenario is a stakeholder-based game. Each stakeholder group has differing needs and views of what sustainability means to them.

Is your business sustainable?

You may have noticed that the term sustainability is used in multiple ways. And that what sustainability means depends on the stakeholder. Let's map this out for clarity.

The stakeholder perspective

Here is a handy frame of reference:

Is your business sustainable, version #1? When customers, partners, and employees ask you this, they want to know what your business is doing to be sustainable. Increasingly, they'll ask for your pledge, plan, and progress—which includes both short-term and long-term components. For these stakeholders, long term means: will the world be in good shape for them in their old age, or, further out, for their grandchildren?

Is your business sustainable, version #2? When asked by Company House in the UK, ACRA in Singapore, and ASIC in Australia because you are submitting your annual report and financial returns, this question is about cash flow and your ability to pay your bills as and when they fall due. This is called the "**going concerns**" test.

In Singapore, there is no official definition for how long you, as a director, think your business will be a going concern. Accounting practice uses 12 months as a reference point. So as a director, you are signing off that your business is robust enough to survive the swings and arrows of outrageous fortune for 12 months from the date of your annual report. Your external auditor will be looking at this from the date of your AGM. This is short-term sustainability. The going concern test is about short-term survival.

Is your business sustainable, version #3? When asked by an investor and by employees who have a long-term interest in the company, this question is about the big-picture view of value creation. Let's call this **strategic sustainability**.

The time frame perspective

Time frames vary significantly. Through the lens of a C-suite team for which I was working on a long-range plan (LRP) recently, three years was the long run. For the regional C-suite, the long run was ten years. For boards working with varied investors, time frames will vary significantly—as we discussed earlier in *the tragedy of the horizon* section in Part 1. Get clear on your investors' mandates and their horizons.

Investors expect there to be value going forward at the end of their investment horizon. This is critical, or else the exit value of their investment is zero.

Exit value expectations

Contingent risks, contingent liabilities, and potential opportunities are all items that are factored into exit valuation. The point of due diligence (DD) process is to discover and discount the valuation for dangers to dividends. DD also looks at the organization's ability to respond and drive future direction of an industry.

While I was running the Financial Services consulting practice at PricewaterhouseCoopers, we referred to DD as finding the buried bodies. If elements of the business model showed future weaknesses or risks, the business model's valuation would be reduced. If there were unrecognized opportunities, also known as undervalued assets, we'd delight. While we'd not mention this to the potential target/purchasee/acquisition/investment, we'd factor the value of these opportunities into our willingness to negotiate price or terms.

Exit value time horizon

Investors with a mandate of five years or more have significant interests in your answer to version #1 of the sustainability question (what are you doing to be sustainable?) and in your value chain's Scope 1, 2, and 3. Behind the demand by investors for ESG reporting lies the fact that investors want to know the quality of the assets they are holding—and the implications to exit valuations or long-term dividend streams.

Family offices, pension funds, and long-term sovereign wealth funds operating a hold strategy are particularly focused on sustainability of profit (the dividends). They know future profits will be affected the degree to which a business model is able to adapt and transition a world that is under +1.5°C.

Going beyond the time frame of investor mandates, investment managers have a fiduciary duty with several elements. One is to ensure returns commensurate to asset class. Another is to consider investor interests. For long-term investors, this time horizon includes the quality of the world that the investor, for example a pensioner, will plan to be alive for in the next few decades.

Aligning interests

There is strategic value in the 2030, 2040, and 2050 lens for us as directors in appreciating both our fiduciary duty as directors and the exit value lens of investors.

This alignment of answers to *Is your business sustainable, versions #1–3* is good news, as it helps us, as directors, shift our perspective and square the circle of historically competing interests of customers, employees, suppliers, and shareholders to what can become a strategically aligned set of collaborative interests.

This leads us to the next key stakeholder: you.

As a director

Is your business sustainable, version #4? This is the question we ask ourselves, as company directors.

Either expressly or implicitly, we are asking, "How long do we want this company to live?" It's a lifespan question. Our fiduciary duty as a board member is to look after the life of the company.

Are you clear what you intend the lifespan of your company to be? Investors, whom one loves and respect, may come and go. Even directors may come and go, when our term limits arise. In Singapore, it's a maximum term of nine years before shareholders further renew three-year terms.

A company set up and run for the purpose of being wound up in the next five years has a very different view of sustainability, capital investment, and future readiness than a company that intends to last 20, 50, or 100+ years.

This is where strategic sustainability is about culture, strategy, and your business model's resilience, adaptability, and agility.

Align horizons

Put financial stakeholders, employees, and human beings on the same page to help align time horizons.

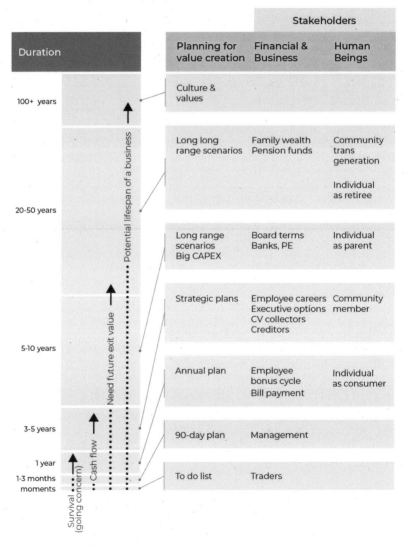

Figure 8 Aligning stakeholder time horizons

As leaders, we have multiple time horizons—all of which align to actions we take now in order to create the future.

As leaders, we determine whether our strategy, decisions, and actions are designed for a rusty future or a green future.

Are you trading while unsustainable?

As directors, we know we have legal liability and can't trade when the company is insolvent. Our company must pass the going concerns test as a basic condition for a continued license to operate.

In the not-too-distant future, we may also need to say we are not trading while unsustainable.

The new sustainability expectations of today are rapidly turning into a norm, table stakes as we go into 2023 and 2024. This has implications for the business as a *going concern* that 12- to 18-month horizon and for *strategic sustainability* over the medium term (5-8 years) as well as for multi-decade, long-term time horizons.

The imperative for strategic sustainability for your business will depend on two significant factors: the speed at which your stakeholders' expectations are changing and the significance those expectations have to your business model. The former sets the pace at which your strategic plans need to move and the later sets the scale of your transformation.

Stakeholder pressure implications

Assess your stakeholders. What is the cumulative trend direction toward which they are pushing your business? A small push from one, added to a nudge from another, plus a shove from a third, and you may feel like you're being buffeted by varied winds. However, once you are clear on their overall direction of travel, as a board you can consider what the appropriate strategic response should be.

1	2	3	4
You have no stakeholder pressures from any of your stakeholders to change.	You see some stakeholders exerting pressure. Nothing significant enough to consider material. All their needs are addressable with minor tweaks to current business operations.	You see multiple stakeholder groups shifting towards sustainability or one major stakeholder creating pressure. Responding to this pressure may require material changes in your business model or your value chain. Addressing these may take longer than current (2–3 year) timelines.	You see substantial needs for sustainability driven action, resulting from your own values or stakeholder pressure. You are redesigning your value chain, aware that implementing some changes will take longer than current (2–3 year) timelines.

Stakeholder Pressure Impact Scale

PART 3

SUSTAINABILITY READINESS: ARE YOU FUTURE-FIT?

Is your business model strategically sustainable?

An organization's overall responsiveness can be defined by their position against the two key factors we outlined above:

1. The future impact of sustainability on the organization's business model

    See *Greensight* Part 1

2. The significance of sustainability to material stakeholders

    See *Greensight* Part 2

This provides a practical framework by which organizational leaders can assess and evaluate the status of their own organizational actions towards sustainability, as shown in Figure 9.

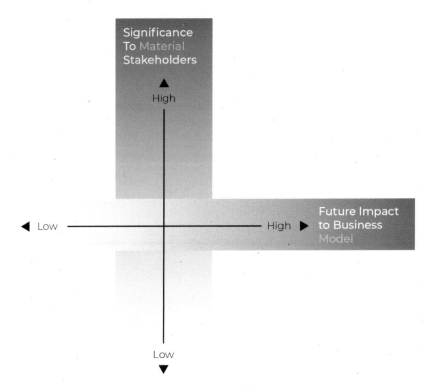

Figure 9 Sustainability responsiveness framework

Sustainability requirements are a relatively new but unavoidable business disruptor. New playbooks are needed to guide senior decision-making.

You can look to organizations that have trod this path. Sustainability-driven businesses are not new.

For example: Olam in Singapore is a global agribusiness that sets sustainability as a distinguishing characteristic. They actively trace and report on Scope 3 impacts. Their sustainability reporting wins awards—one judge told me their transparency in linking standards to metrics leads the pack.

German car manufacturer BMW has expanded sustainability from cars that last a long time to designing for circularity in its products, and a public commitment to a 40% carbon reduction by 2030, along with commitments and standards that include Tier 2 suppliers.

Interface, a global carpet tiling company from the USA, shifted from pure profit-driven business model to sustainability-driven, profit-based business in 1994 and has had multiple stages in its journey to get to net zero emissions across seven pillars of sustainability. They call this Mission Zero®. Once they achieved this, they set forth on their Climate Take Back™ ambition, with a regenerative target.

The Sustainability Responsiveness Framework provides a road map with which leaders can assess, evaluate, and shift the status of their own organizational actions towards sustainability.

Organizations fall into one of four "sustainability responsiveness" typologies, based on the nature and degree of their responsiveness strategy to the sustainability imperative.

Generally speaking, organizations operating towards the rusty scenario leaned to the left in this schema, while organization with green scenario ambitions and pledges to net zero, true zero and restorative operations leaned to the right side.

The typologies of sustainability responsiveness

Within this typology are four strategic sustainability responses.

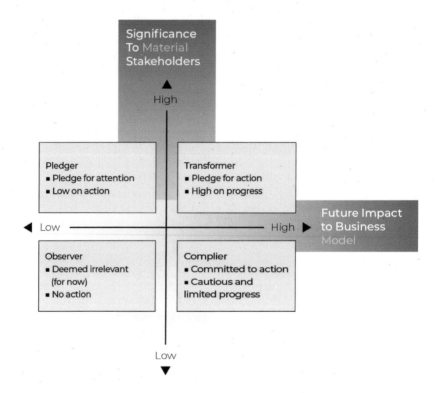

Figure 10 Sustainability responsiveness profiles

Clearly, each profile in this typology has its strategic validity in terms of leadership. Assessments are what make your strategic response defendable.

These are the four Sustainability Responsiveness Profiles. Each profile takes a distinct view of what strategic sustainability is to them and six dynamics that those boards consider important.

You can use this typology as an informal self-assessment of where your business is currently and where you think it may need to be in the near future. Go to GreensightGuide.com/assessment for a more detailed report on your topology. More on this in the next section.

The Observer

The observer is appropriate for businesses that see no need to change.

As a board, you respond this way because none of the following stakeholders are expecting sustainability from you:

- Customers
- Employees
- Investors
- Suppliers
- Regulators
- Society.

You as a board assess your strategic fitness to deliver profitably in a net-zero world with no changes required. You will also need to confirm that no changes will flow from changes in your value chain for this to have substance.

Your strategic transformation plan does not require a sustainability plan.

If this is the case, you can say with confidence that your business model will last—under the assumption that your company will be creating value for the next 5–10 years.

The six characteristics of the Sustainability Observer are:

1. Focuses on traditional business as usual, operational efficiency, profit maximization

2. Believes that the sector is not exposed to immediate or medium-term sustainability risk

3. Does not perceive stakeholders to be driving immediate or significant change

4. Has no stated commitments or plans, but may be monitoring and assessing external trends

5. Adopting a wait-and-see approach towards regulation

6. Change averse, with culture of *preserving the status quo.*

The Pledger

The Pledger is appropriate for businesses where there is a need to express direction of ambition.

As a board, you respond this way because some of the following stakeholders are expecting some level of sustainability from you:

- Customers
- Employees
- Investors
- Suppliers
- Regulators
- Society.

You will need to make the necessary commitments that these stakeholders require to remain committed to you, or at least so they do to not create enterprise risk issues.

It will also be because you as a board have assessed your strategic fitness to deliver profitably in a net-zero world with no changes required. You will also need to confirm that no changes will flow from shifts in your value chain for this to have substance.

Your strategic transformation plan is independent of your sustainability plan. The later may be managed as an add-on to a current strategic initiative or as a stand-alone project.

If this is the case, you can say with confidence that your business model will last—under the assumption that your company will be creating value for the next 5–10 years.

The six characteristics of the Sustainability Pledger are:

1. Sees that sector is on the brink of significant change, in medium- to long-term future

2. Aware of changing demands of stakeholders

3. Committed to maintain self-determination and evolving ahead of regulatory pressure

4. Has long-range public commitments, focusing on Scope 1/ carbon neutral/offsetting

5. In the process of preparing a response plan and is conducting measurement, but this is yet to be translated into enterprise-wide actions

6. Responsibility for change delegated to operational leaders with limited action on the deep levers of change.

The Complier

The Complier is appropriate for businesses where there is an actionable, present-time need for action.

As a board, you respond this way because some of the following stakeholders are expecting data, plans, and progress on sustainability at some level from you:

- Customers
- Employees
- Investors
- Suppliers
- Regulators
- Society.

You will need to make the necessary commitments and to show that you are delivering on them so that these stakeholders remain committed to you, or at least so they do to not create enterprise risk issues.

It will also be because you as a board have assessed your strategic fitness to deliver profitably in a net-zero world and identified that some changes are required.

You will also need to confirm that only financially immaterial changes will flow from shifts in your value chain for this to have substance.

You may also have determined that some changes will result from shifts in your value chain, and you will have integrated the implications of these into your strategic plan so that your strategic plan is sustainable.

Your strategic transformation plan and your sustainability plan are aligned but managed separately.

If this is the case, you can say with confidence that your business model will last—under the assumption that your company will be creating value for the next 5–10 years.

The six characteristics of the Sustainability Complier are:

1. Clear that sector is on the brink of significant change, in the near to medium-term future

2. Stakeholder assessment focuses on short-term opportunity—capital market disclosure, customer procurement

3. Sustainability response is in place, but relatively siloed, without strong integration with corporate mission

4. Visions and plans are in place addressing Scopes 1 and 2 with focus on risk and damage mitigation

5. On the leader's agenda there is some delegation to sustainability officers, marketing, operations, etc.

6. Business model adjustments, measurement, and reporting systems are typically focused on compliance/external reports.

The Transformer

The Transformer is appropriate for businesses where there is a purposeful or significant present-time need for action.

As a board, you respond this way because some of the following stakeholders are expecting significant data, plans, and progress on sustainability from you:

- Customers
- Employees
- Investors
- Suppliers
- Regulators
- Society.

You will need to make the necessary commitments and to show that you are delivering them so that these stakeholders remain committed to you, and so that they do not create enterprise risk issues.

This may be self-motivated, as both board and company have identified your values and purpose to be aligned to a net-zero or regenerative ambition.

Your transformative actions also stem from the fact that you as a board have assessed your strategic fitness to deliver profitably in a net-zero world and identified that some changes are required or that significant changes are required urgently.

You will also need to confirm that only changes that are financially immaterial will flow from shifts in your value chain for this to have substance.

You may also have determined that significant impacts will result from changes in your value chain.

This means you have a robust 5- and 10-year transformation program in action—and you have confidence in its ability to deliver.

Your strategic transformation plan and your sustainability plan are one and the same.

If this is the case, you can say with confidence that your business model will last—under the assumption that your company will be creating value for the next 5–10 years.

The six characteristics of the Sustainability Transformer are:

1. Clear understanding of the changing nature of all stakeholder priorities and needs, and the nature of the associated risks and opportunities

2. Addressing business model changes are seen as imperative to the longevity of the organization

3. Ambitious regenerative Scope 3 vision, over narrow and defensive "do less harm" goals

4. Sustainability is baked into board and C-Suite agendas, integrated into business strategy and culture

5. Sustainability pledge, plan and progress are made public and leveraged to attract talent, investment, suppliers, and customers

6. Extensively using all levers of sustainability responsiveness: leadership agenda, ambition of assessment, and ambition of response.

How do each of these types see strategic sustainability?

From the perspective of the **Observer**, strategic sustainability is irrelevant. To the **Pledger**, it's optional—nice to have, but nothing more. For the **Complier**, it is seen as necessary, so they'll do what it takes to ensure the required boxes are ticked, standards are met, and license to operate with each stakeholder will be maintained. The **Transformer** sees strategic sustainability as a critical element to their mission and a necessity for medium-term value creation. They are also more likely see and invest in value creation options.

Chairman Larry Fink of major investor Blackrock believes the next thousand unicorns won't be search engines or social media companies, they'll be sustainable, scalable innovators, startups that help the world decarbonize and make the energy transition affordable for all consumers. And established companies can play the sustainability unicorn game, too.

Now, what do *you* need to do to be ready for strategic sustainability? Strategic sustainability becomes a reality when your business is has the right sustainability responsiveness profile for the challenges of the pressures that are coming. With the pace of change coming from stakeholders, boards and C-suites will need to ensure their governance is able to deliver to these future needs.

Regardless of where your organization currently sits in the typology above, who needs to do what so that your sustainability governance delivers what you need?

PART 4

BOARD ACTION

Responsibility and Liabilities

To swiftly recap earlier sections, sustainability demands on businesses are evolving rapidly, in ways that are complex and multifaceted. For the proactive business leader, this presents opportunities. Responsibilities are shifting across and within organizations, in part due to the value chain perspective of Scope 3 and in part due to stakeholder pressure.

The changes coming from the Scope 3 value-chain perspective and stakeholder pressures can be distilled into three big questions:

1. What are you doing to sustainability?
2. What is sustainability doing to you?
3. What are you going to do about (1) and (2)?

What is clear today is that a trend for increased transparency and accountability across stakeholders is showing up in the USA, Australia, UK, the EU, Singapore, Malaysia, and Hong Kong.

In Singapore the Corporate Code of Governance applies to all company directors and expects them to take into account the interests of other stakeholders. The Singapore Stock Exchange and the Singapore Institute of Directors consider sustainability sufficiently important that it is a compulsory topic for all directors that serve on a listed board.

Note: In China, business tends follow and conform to directives of the Communist Party. Keep this in mind for any operations, subsidiaries, and growth plans involving Chinese partners.

Customer-driven sustainability?

As a commercial enterprise, you may question if customers are willing to pay more for sustainability-based products or services. They may not be. However, sustainability has table stakes. In a business owner survey, 100% said that all things being equal, they'd buy services from the company with a sustainability record over one without. A bank that I do business with asks for sustainability statements and verification of potential new partners. Four months ago, they didn't. Just because customers are not demanding sustainability accountability yet, does not mean they won't in the very near future.

This reenforces the importance of agility and adaptability as core business competencies.

Hyper-granular data and AI will drive transparency and accountability

By 2024, expect that external parties will be able to report on your performance, thanks to integration of geographic information systems (GIS) that integrate logistics, on-the-ground actions, and blockchain.

Science fiction or fact? An insurance company can rate the insurance risk of an individual businesses based on which side of the street they are located, employee engagement, and customer feedback with a predictive capacity to price insurance. This existed in Myanmar in 2019. The next layer for social and environmental impact was delayed by the COVID-19 pandemic and local political stability issues.

Smart money is betting on predictive AI to identify hot spots for social action. In some cases, Twitter is already doing an effective job with #namingandshaming. Anticipate that investors and other stakeholders will look to these and other tech sources for independent data verification.

S&P's purchase and integration of TrueCost is a signal that ratings agencies see long-term value from independent ESG-based data on actual business performance.

Boards with foresight gain long term value from sustainability. Those that proactively invest have leverageable capacities.

> For example: Unilever, a pillar of the European food industry, revitalized its business in 2010 with their Sustainable Living Plan with a series of ambitious targets, including improving the lives of a billion people. A decade on, they report progress—

and how far they believe they have to go. This acknowledged, Unilever is ahead of most businesses in terms of capacities, relationships, and credibility. Their goal is net zero in Scope 1 by 2030 and net zero across Scope 3 by 2039.[28]

Australian integrated real estate and investment group Lendlease uses sustainability as a core part of its decision-making framework. This has led to awards, expertise, and an ability to deliver financially, socially, and environmentally. Their framework is refreshed regularly to retain relevance, most recently in 2019. They share their learnings on the net-zero carbon journey, aiming for net zero by 2025 and absolute (true) zero carbon by 2030 across Scope 1, 2, and 3 emissions in Europe.[29]

Businesses like these and others are acting like Transformers. They know things that the Observers, Pledgers, and Compliers don't—anticipate that businesses that pick up Transformer capacities will accelerate impact and returns in the next decade.

Legal reality regardless of your capital structure

Even if you are not listed on a stock exchange or looking for funds from the capital markets, you still have legal exposure.

---

28 *Unilever Climate Transition Action Plan,* 22 March 2021. This report includes their insights on what works, thanks to their decade of investment in the Unilever Sustainable Living Plan. See more: https://assets.unilever.com/files/92ui5egz/production/bbe89d14aa9e0121dd3a2b9721bbfd3bef57b8d3.pdf/unilever-climate-transition-action-plan-19032021.pdf.

29 https://www.lendlease.com/au/better-places/lendlease-europe-shares-first-progress-update-towards-mission-zero/.

- Long-term sustainability through addressing stakeholder interests applies to all businesses, listed or not. In the USA, you need to be a shareholder to take legal action for violation of stakeholder interests. In Singapore, legal standing may not be limited to shareholders; customers may have standing based on marketing promises made to them. In the UK and Australia, the legal concept of the rights of future generations means that directors can be and are taken to court for the impact of past and present business decisions on the next generation.
- Scope 3 levels the field in that enterprises choosing to use third-party businesses to manage risk and exposure will retain accountability for the impact of their value chain.

SubCos

Subsidiary companies including those developed for legal and risk management (or project entities) are rolled up as part of Scope 1 and 2.

InvestCos

Investment companies, be they PE, VC, sovereign wealth funds, or banks, have the sustainability impact of their investment allocated to their books based on SASB.

ListCos

Listed companies must issue sustainability reports to the exchange. In Singapore, these have the same standing as annual reports and financial statements. In other words, as a director, you are legally responsible for statements, including the forward-looking statements that relate to sustainability.

Early in 2022, the SGX issued a consultation paper on the content of sustainability reports. In true Singapore style, the paper is actually a heads-up about the reporting that the SGX will expect in the very near future (see Appendix: Nine Board Sustainability Q&As for a summary of 20 sustainability reporting items.) Data collection takes time and effort. For entities listed in Singapore, get into action—now.

If you are not listed in Singapore, the paper is worth looking at as an indication of future trends. Singapore takes its position as a respected global center for business and finance seriously and sees being a pioneer in sustainability accountability as a part of its future competitive edge.

PrivateCo

Private companies may issue sustainability reports to share what they are doing with stakeholders, as well as their pledge (intentions), their plans, and their progress. The reality is that banks, customers, suppliers, and employees will rely on such statements, expecting substance rather than marketing puffery.

Board Accountabilities

With the increasing pressure for businesses to have substantive sustainability plans, the trend is for organizations to be either Compliers—confident their organization can deliver on net-zero/net-positive goals by 2030 as a condition for license to operate—or Transformers driven by purpose toward the sustainability transformation or at lease having identified substantive business model opportunities beyond net zero.

In practice, many of the elements outlined here will be codeveloped with the CEO and C-suite. However, the buck legally stops with the board. Boards and management will need to update their expectations of accountability oversight and operations so that they can effectively work together in this swift-moving space. In many cases, boards will look to management to create policies that then get built into plans to generate progress. Boards may choose to be involved in this policy creation, seek external insights, or delegate responsibility for policy, pledges, plans, and progress to the CEO and C-suite.

Note that sustainability is not a Rule of 72 environment, nor is it operating according to a predictable rate of change. Boards and management will need an agile and adaptive approach to long-term value creation.

So, who needs to do what so that the business is strategically sustainable?

As it is not easy to begin with a blank piece of paper (even if you have taken great notes as you read this book), this section outlines the major board and board committee roles, including responsibility, liability, and risk profiles, as well as action that each role may take. For for handy printable checklists go to GreensightGuide.com/Checklists

The section following this one focuses on sustainability governance for the board and the Chief Sustainability Officer. The final section of Part 4 focus on C-suite roles—all of which are impacted to some extent by sustainability. Each has a part to play in sustainability governance.

While these three sections are not exhaustive, the contents of this section will speed up your sustainability transition, help refine your sustainability strategy, and assist in creating green mindsets and cultures.

Your business will have its own unique history and facts. What is here is an example for you to adapt for your own business needs. When I facilitate this with leadership teams, the discussion is rich with history, vision, and practical actions.

Board of directors and founder teams

Set the Goal, Maintain the Pace

Responsibility: long-term economic, environmental, and social performance with requisite governance for growth and regulatory compliance.

Liability: civil and criminal responsibility under common law and increasingly under statute law. Delivery of fiduciary duty of care, loyalty. Negligence for inaction in respect to climate-change risks to business.

Risk profile: personal liability risk has increased. Business may face sectoral risks, contingency liabilities, and asset write-downs affecting profit and loss, balance sheets, and potentially cash flow.

While the items below may be delegated to the C-suite and management, a board's responsibility means accountability and oversight of these actions remain with the board.

Action:

Understand shifting landscapes:

- Assess stakeholder interest in sustainability and anticipate future standards and expectations
- Determine future scenarios over a 20-year horizon to ensure exit value over the 5, 10, and 15-year timelines
- Back-cast what the 20-year horizon could mean to your value chain, considering resilience/survival and transition planning
- Articulate what changes to culture and tone from the top will be required to deliver on your sustainability strategy
- Identify which of the four sustainability typologies (Observer, Pledger, Complier, or Transformer) is appropriate for your business

Set goal—your pledge

- For example: net zero by 2030 across Scopes 1, 2, and 3
- Recommendation: use science-based targets
- Sequence and prioritize action based on its impact to your value chain
- Select the framework/standards your company will use for disclosure

Acknowledge your position

- Know where you are currently across each of the eight environment elements, seven social elements, and eight governance elements (see pages 58-62 on underactioned ESG criteria)

- Define if board oversight needs ensure results are investor grade
- Ensure that your sustainability narrative across stakeholders is coherent and consistent
- Disclose where you are across the ESG elements and demonstrate that you are using the appropriate communications platform

Define strategic sustainability plan

- Identify leading indicator KPIs for board-level tracking
- Fund and approve transformation plan to deliver pledge and stakeholder commitments
- Establish clear milestones to mark progress
- Better practice: integrate sustainability plans with other strategic actions into one plan so that trade-offs are recognized

Director's insurance:

- Ensure your D&O policy covers you for actions and inactions in terms of climate and other sustainability risks
- Note: insurance companies are revising what they consider insurable

Committee charters

- Decide if the board will manage ESG reporting considerations
- Update committee charters
- Define disclosure policy for stakeholders for transparency on sustainability

Annually:

- Recognize shifts in stakeholder norms
- Review progress
- Refine strategic sustainability plan

Audit committee (AC)

Ensure Rigor: Disclosure, Messaging and Metrics

Accountable oversight:

- Ensure adequacy of data and controls to reduce risks while enabling opportunity
- Set disclosure, data, and controls policy for strategic sustainability
- Track and escalate variance in progress through metrics
- Review and if material, seek independent assurance of data used in sustainability disclosures
- Proactively require asset quality and value chain robustness over the 5- and 10-year horizons
- Assess implications of contingent liabilities to financial position
- Monitor third-party ratings to ensure position to peers is competitively appropriate to strategy (In other words, do you decide to follow, track to norms, or lead?)
- Evaluate alignment of sustainability messaging through organization and across stakeholders
- Ensure adequate processes and controls so that disclosures are accurate, comparable, and consistent

Risk committee (BRC)

Navigate Volatility

Accountable oversight:

- Incorporate sustainability risks across the ESG dimensions into enterprise risk management
- Set risk policy for strategic sustainability
- Ensure that robust external data and research-based science informs risk assessment
- Preemptively review culture to ensure it is a good fit with your purpose
- Include assessments based on lead-time in risk profiling so that you have adequate response time to address risks
- Flag challenges to meeting commitments that arise from meeting a chosen framework or standard
- Balance risk mitigation with opportunity enablement for 5, 10, and 15-year value horizons

Nominations and governance committee (NC)

Right People, Right Purpose, Right Action

Accountable oversight:

- Evaluate stakeholder understanding and insights so that nuances are swiftly incorporated to board agenda
- Enable director understanding and skills sets on ESG oversight efforts
- Set culture and people policy for strategic sustainability

- Align tone from the top so that leaders ensure an appropriate sustainability culture throughout the organization
- Assess governance and delegations so that each division/leader has required authority for action
- Evaluate leadership and resulting risk culture to assure appropriate pace of change for organization
- Review succession planning, nominations, and governance so that forward talent pipeline is a good fit for your purpose
- Ensure top-to-toe understanding of sustainability and ESG throughout the organization
- Enable a success and highlights process so that early actors and success stories are used for learning and leverage (like positive whistle blowers)

Renumeration committee (RC)

Reward Right Action

Accountable oversight:

- Ensure sustainability goals and milestones from the strategy are effectively built into executive compensation
- Evaluate rewards, compensation, and benefits to ensure alignment of sustainability accountability processes
- Review HR policies so that the decision-making practices for reviews, career planning, and promotions reenforce the sustainability strategy
- Ensure compensation and benefits align with culture, risk, and controls policies set by other board committees

Sustainability Governance

Sustainability committee (SC)

Integrate sustainability and strategy

Proactive boards are establishing sustainability committees to address the complex interaction of financial, environmental, social, and governance elements.

Ensure this committee's mandate is clear—whether it's as advisory to the board, with its job to understand and recommend direction, or if the action and key decision-making will be centered here in this committee. As this committee has a strong strategic focus, the boundary between it and the full board will need to be clear.

With the board, identify which category from the Sustainability Responsiveness Typology is appropriate for your business, given the long-term time horizon you set for your business's longevity and legacy. Be clear that your business is either an Observer, a Pledger, a Complier, or a Transformer.

Strategic sustainability response depends on where you are now (your current assessment) and where you determine the business needs to get to in the future.

There are specific levers that organizations can apply to drive their positions forward and which—taken together—determine their overall responsiveness to the pressures sustainability is putting on business.

1. Leadership agenda
2. Ambition of assessment
3. Ambition of response

Work with your CSO to ensure that across the organization, actions are appropriate and aligned. You will want this role to be a neutral, strategic player who, like a good sports coach, makes sure the business team plays the game you have set. While both internal auditors and the CSO have reporting lines to the board, the former are focused on ensuring regulatory compliance is delivered on while the CSO focuses on delivery on the sustainability strategy.

Let's look at the CSO role before turning to the levers you can use to address the imperative of your organization's sustainability responsiveness.

Chief Sustainability Officer (SCO)

This is a new role in most organizations. Fundamentally, an empowered CSO's challenge is to maintain the strategic sustainability lens. It's to balance the need to grow with not blowing up. Get the balance wrong and over time, you'll be rolled into compliance for reporting and HR for training. Or simply relegated to marketing as a Pledger.

If this role does not report to the board as an independent line of insight, boards and C-suites will find that past practices—firmly rooted in the rusty scenario—will dominate. Without deliberate action to change, the organization will find little reason to shift decision-making, culture, and behavior and default to what worked in the past. The Sustainability Surge suggests this may be a high-risk option.

Behind any successful green scenario shift is a leadership decision to focus on winning deep. Winning deep uses the assets you already have to put your ambition into action. Organizations that thrive see change as the new normal and build capacities to continually adapt. They focus on systems, not silos. Leaders that win deep create legacies, not liabilities.

As CSO, you are key to the green scenario—and your organization's success.

Assess and act	Stakeholders to engage
Based on your Sustainability Responsiveness Typology (Observer, Pledger, Complier, Transformer), your role will vary	C-suite, CEO, board (See this as a multi-dimensional matrix to ensure independence and integration)

Ask

- What do your pledge and strategy represent to maintaining the business as a going concern and for strategic sustainability?
- What short-term action is necessary to align interests across internal and external stakeholders?
- What board/C-suite engagement will be needed so that leadership is aligned and resources are available?

Act

- Evaluate the organization's ability to align divergent interests so that these can be addressed early
- Specify the target for growth and compliance so that sustainability is value generation, not a penalty
- Identify the support and resources you will need for stakeholder management, internally and externally

Challenges to address

- Continually: alignment of actions and KPIs to forward-looking scenarios, pledge, and science-based targets
- Short term: review enterprise actions for rigor and credibility to ensure these are appropriate, given your pledge
- Short to medium term: establish coherent narrative around sustainability and business value that is then embedded in the organization. With the board, set roles, responsibilities, and relationships that allow dynamic realignment to business outcomes and strategic sustainability

Sustainability responsiveness levers

What is clear is that in general, organizations are in the early stages of responding to the Sustainability Surge. Early adopting Transformers provide insight into the levers they are engaging for organizational transformation, sharing them along with 2022 uptake rates. Use the levers to accelerate pace of change and alignment. This is particularly important for Transformers and Compliers.

Leadership agenda

Two key questions determine the single most important lever of change, which is organizational leadership:

1. To what extent are leaders driving sustainability change in their actions?
2. How have they established ownership and accountability across the organization?

In the *Imperative of Sustainability Responsiveness* report,[30] our research revealed a wide range of responses with respect to how sustainability sits with the leadership agenda here in Asia.

Extracts from this report are included in grey boxes below so that you can benchmark your organization with others here.

> Given the importance of sustainability as an issue, it is no surprise that it is on the leadership agenda, with 96% of organizations confirming that the need for a sustainability strategy is on the radar—to some extent. But the strength and urgency of the signal varies considerably.
>
> The question is the extent to which leaders are actively driving change in their organizations.
>
> Are they walking the talk?
>
> - 45% of leaders say the organization is "walking the talk," with enterprise-wide action being undertaken
> - 40% say they're "talking but not yet walking;" as yet there is no coherent strategy
> - 15% admitted "some talk, no walk;" no meaningful commitments or actions to date.
>
> For some organizations, ownership sits at the very top. For most others, ownership is diffused or delegated.

30 Flinn, J., Wilson, A. *The Imperative of Sustainability Responsiveness*. 2022. Walking the collaboration talk myself: working with Andy Wilson, who is the Head of Sustainability at Ogilvy, to analyze the survey responses and refine the Sustainability Responsiveness typologies was brilliant. Our perspectives differ, yet by integrating our views we developed something more powerful for you.

One of the strongest signals of the pace and breadth of organization transformation is the degree to which top leaders own accountability and responsibility of the issue.

- 41% said this issue sits with the very top (board and CEO)
- 50% say sustainability ownership extends to a range of other functions. Within this group, 35% said it sits with a Chief Sustainability Officer
- 9% said there was no formal allocation of responsibility.

Ambition of assessment

Sustainability-driven transformation has three aspects:

- Strategic fitness over the 5-10 year and then 20-year horizon so that you are fit for the future (which means tracking to where the future will be, not aiming to be where the others were last year)
- Ability to respond and adapt to transition issues (the impacts of changes on environment and assets, communities, and value chains)
- The transformation needed to address stakeholder-based leadership, reduce risks, and actually deliver on pledges. This is about progress, metrics and yes, disclosure.

Ambition of response

But assessment of external factors is one thing—an organization's actions are the only way in which meaningful progress will be made. We call this the sustainability journey, and it follows three universal steps, or the 3Ps of Sustainability:

Step 1: It begins with ambition—the organization's **pledge** or promise towards a sustainable future.

Step 2: Then, a road map—the milestone **plan** of how to get there.

Step 3: Followed by action, measurement, and disclosure of **progress.**

Remember, it's not where you are on the journey that matters, but the nature of the journey you have chosen—starting with your pledge.

The 3 Ps of Sustainability

The Pledge

Be crystal clear so that your organization knows what it needs to deliver. As a board, set your ambition. Pick what is most appropriate for your Sustainability Responsiveness Profile.

Here's a handy list of the components your pledge should cover:

Your ambition:
(Pick one of these three)

- Limiting global temperature rise to under +1.5°C for a green future
- Limiting global rise to 3°, aligns with COP26 promises and puts our future in the rusty red world

- Accepting +7° increases as inevitable—a dark rusty world, defaulting to historical practices and a fossil fuel-based economy

Carbon and greenhouse gases:
(pick one of these)

- Regenerative (removing past CO_2)
- True zero (no CO_2 emitted)
- Net zero (some CO_2 emitted but offset)
- Reduce intensity or absolute amount
- Await regulation

By when
(pick your date)

- 2030
- 2040
- 2050
- At some stage

To what extent
(identify the scope you are reporting on)

- Scope 1: just our own direct impact
- Scope 2: including the energy we need
- Scope 3: incorporating our entire value chain

Note: many organizations have strict Scope 1 goals for themselves and broader Scope 3 goals that recognize their relative ability to influence their value chain.

It's also important to state goals recognizing impact on/usage of the other five impact categories:

- Biodiversity and land use
- Water and marine resources
- Pollution and waste
- Communities and well-being
- Engagement in circular economy.

Given the interrelationships between these five impact categories and carbon, expect to identify more than one pathway to your overall ambition.

Your preferred pathway will be determined by your organization's culture and values, along with the financial scenarios that these pathways generate. Your preferred pathways will be based on where you see your stakeholders and business model evolve. Incorporate future macro-events and trends. You may find that some parts of your business value chain are Compliers, while others may be Transformers.

Note: if your business has multiple brands, a brand with low ambition may become the weak link in your sustainability strategy. Accountability for sustainability is at the board level, not the brand level.

> *Accountability for sustainability is at the board level, not the brand level.*

As important is it is for boards and directors to be aware of sustainability and to set company strategy for long-term sustainability, it's also increasingly necessary for everyone in your organization to understand these considerations, too. Otherwise, they won't be making informed, aligned decisions at operational levels.

Your sustainability ambition may or may not be something that you choose to share externally. However, customers are likely to ask you for your ambition or goal or pledge—if not now, then in the very near future.

An organization's pledge serves an important purpose in creating a weight of action and accountability to external stakeholders. Capital markets and investors are increasingly reviewing a company's position according to the ambition and credibility of its pledge.

Internally, the ambition of the pledge is a critical indicator of future action. Organizations with no stated pledge are unlikely to make significant plans or take significant actions. Conversely, organizations with ambitious pledges stand the most chance of galvanizing the imagination and resources required to actually achieve that ambition.

Our survey of executives in Asia found:

- **No pledge ambition: 39%** of organizations surveyed had no committed climate target
- **Do no harm ambition: 45%** were committed to act toward under +1.5°C, with a net-zero pledge. Net zero is now table stakes
- **Regenerative ambition: 15%** of organizations were committed to net positive, which means carbon contributions of the past are progressively cleaned up. This is becoming the norm for high performers.

The pace

Be clear about which sustainability elements you are focusing on—and when you hope to achieve those goals. Based on your business scale and industry, certain components of sustainability will be necessary:

- This year
- Next year
- The following year
- Beyond

Some sustainability elements will require lead times before they can be put in place. Understand how this will play out for your business, and factor in the uncertainties of present-day global issues including war, famine, pandemics, and technology in the form of digitalization, AI, and robotics.

In addition, the pace of regulation appears to be picking up. Where stock exchanges and central banks used to give businesses three years to get organized when a significant new regulation like Know Your Customer or Anti-Bribery was rolled out, they now are allowing a year. They understand is that time is of the essence.

Stakeholders are also shifting their expectations faster.

In 2019, it was the rare Request for Proposal (RFP) that asked about sustainability practices. By end of 2021, over 50% of RFPs requested this information. As of Q1,'22, that number is now at 75%.

Banks didn't ask about ESG a few years ago. In 2022, transparency around ESG reporting will be the norm in fundraising activities.

All of these suggest businesses that proactively build capacity for adaptability and agility will be better positioned to respond, change, and grow than those that play catch-up.

Plan

A promise or a goal without a plan is vaporware. Begin with a road map that allows you to express how you can implement sustainability in your proposed timeframes. Build a strategy for change and resilience.

The most effective sustainability plans are those that:

1. Provide a clear road map and milestones for progress to the public pledge
2. Are socialized across the whole enterprise, so that everyone is clear and motivated about what is required
3. Are visible in order to drive accountability, improve credibility, and accelerate collaboration and alignment across your value chain.

If you've yet to start, do not despair. Many organizations are just beginning the journey, too.

Our *Imperative of Sustainability Responsiveness* respondents shared the nature and readiness of their sustainability plans:

- **Plans not ready: 60%** reported having no structure for measurable public accountability. This may signal either that sustainability is not an issue for the organization or that they are in the early stages of getting their heads (and thus actions) around what is a complex issue. Unless they take action, these organizations are likely to face significant commercial risks in the near future.

- **A plan is in place: 15%** reported the presence of a plan that was widely understood within the organization. A plan without awareness and understanding won't deliver results. This is the foundational position for delivery of either compliance needs or growth opportunities to external stakeholders.

- **A plan that is owned and put into action: 23%** have plans that are widely understood and acted upon. These organizations are successfully taking on creating awareness and understanding of the plan and the role sustainability plays in business success.

The robustness of an organization's sustainability plan can be gauged by how deeply it drives change across its structural arrangements. Specifically, does the plan require a change of investment practices, and does the plan include suppliers and partners across the value chain?

We used two litmus tests to explore the robustness of plans.

Investment practices

Forty-one percent of leaders confirmed that investments are still made solely on the basis of financial returns, with no consideration of impact on sustainability. It is unlikely these organizations will allocate sufficient funding to make the necessary changes.

The remaining 59% are actively incorporating sustainability criteria into investment decisions, either as on par with financial returns (28%) or as a filter before financial considerations (31%).

Partners and supply chain

Just 33% of organizations actively selected suppliers based on sustainability credentials, while 53% saw sustainability credentials as an optional extra. And 14% considered sustainability credentials irrelevant.

Anticipate that this percentage will shift rapidly as organizations take action on Scope 3 commitments.

Progress

Privately measured progress is passé. Sustainability will thrive under public quantification and scrutiny.

Nobody denies that sustainability measurement is complex. New quantification protocols are being introduced, which will bring benefits of common definitions and standards, ultimately accelerating transparency.

Our respondents were at different stages on this journey to transparency.

- **Not begun: 25%** had not gotten started.
- **Measured by not disclosed: 25%** were actively collecting data, but they were not yet confident enough to report this data externally.
- **Public disclosure: 22%** are reporting externally to stakeholders but are yet to have independently verified data. Organizations will increasingly be asked for assurance of data quality, measurement appropriateness, and rigor.
- **Publicly disclosed and independently verified accountability: 18.5%** are substantiating reports with independent verification, while some of the 18.5% provide reporting on Scope 3 impact.

Priorities

What gets measured gets done, what gets rewarded gets prioritized

How many organizations are actually aligning and rewarding performance to sustainability targets? KPIs, compensation, and benefits integrated into career planning are proven means for ensuring aligned business action.

We asked whether sustainability performance was being reflected in pay and career prospects among the top 10% of employees—a strong signal that sets the tone from the top, drives cross-functional alignment, and defines corporate culture.

What we found reflects the current maturity of many businesses in their sustainability journey.

- **Not yet tied: 45%** of organizations have made no link between sustainability performance and rewards/career prospects. Traditional shareholder business culture is likely to perpetuate in these organizations and may lead to long-term culture risks.
- **Loosely linked: 34%** say there is a loose link between pay, career opportunities, and sustainability performance. This may not create the pace of change needed over the next three to eight years.
- **Tightly aligned: 21%** show alignment between what's pledged by the company and the KPIs, rewards, and performance of its people.

The proof

Regardless of whether your business has decided to commit to a climate pledge, regardless of whether you've developed a robust strategy and plan that incorporates sustainability, you'll be asked for proof.

In Singapore, the SGX expects sustainability reports from all listed companies. They are looking for these reports to be assured. These forward-looking statements are as formal a part of board reporting as annual financial reports. The SEC in the USA has announced their listing rules will do likewise.

Thanks to Scope 3 pressures from listed companies, unlisted companies will also need to provide sustainability-based data in the form of reports, certificates, and assurance to standards in order to stay competitive in the value chains of the future.

Insurers and bankers may ask you for sustainability reporting, certification, and assurance—or decline to pay out or do business with you if you can't provide such documentation.

At an even more basic level, sustainability data is increasingly valuable and necessary for being licensed to operate. More and more, businesses will be required to deliver on their sustainability commitments, be these your marketing promises or what you've pledged to your banker, value-chain partners, or the exchange you're listed on.

> For example, the SEC in the USA has fined BNY Mellon Investment Advisors for ESG mis-statements. While this is the first case of it's kind, it will not be the last. Anticipate increasing regulatory focus on probity of statements.

> The Australian Competition and Consumer Commission (ACCC) has indicated that they will be taking a tough approach to businesses "falsely promoting environmental or green credentials to capitalise" on demands that they reduce their environmental footprints—in other words, greenwashing. This will put pressure on Pledgers to shift into one of the other three typologies: Observer, Complier, or Transformer.

All of this make it critical to ensure your leaders and business are aligned to your strategic sustainability direction. So, what does your C-suite need to do?

Enabling executive leadership execution of sustainability strategy

Executing, refining, and recommending

Together with the board, as an executive team, you've answered these questions.

1. What are you doing to sustainability?
2. What is sustainability doing to you?
3. What are you going to do about (1) and (2)?

You've identified the right business typology for your strategy for value creation. And you've worked with the board to align your business's pledge, policies, plans, and progress.

You'll be refreshing your strategy, identifying impacts to your business model, and ensuring the plans you have for strategic sustainability are robust, deliver results, and are flexible enough to do so while navigating our turbulent, uncertain, complex world.

You are the heart and arms of the board in the business. You and your strategy team will be working closely with the board to determine your sustainability strategy. And given the pace that external expectations are shifting, expect to iterate and refine your strategy.

Twin challenges

Your twin challenges: ensuring the practical necessities of keeping the lights on so that the business continues to be a going concern, *and* leading your people so that they buy into the pacing and necessity for sustainability-driven change.

This is no small challenge today. CEOs tell me that they have 35–50% of their renumeration based on sustainability targets, yet they struggle to get their organization to align and take action. This need not be so.

Here is a practical spectrum of action:

- *Keep the Lights On* (KTLO), where focus is on remaining a going concern, license to operate today, and other current commitments
- *Grow the Business* (GTB), where focus is on incremental shifts that add up over time, license to operate next year
- *Transform the Future* (TTF), where action is about distinctive change, delivery of strategy, and long-term value creation. This is what we are calling strategic sustainability, and it ensures license to operate in 2030 and value in 2030.

All C-suite roles have responsibilities that encompass KTLO, GTB, and TTF.

Strategic sustainability is future casting needs. It's seeing where the hockey puck will be. It's understanding the lights under which your success will be judged. And it's getting the right pieces in place now, so that each year you are moving distinctly towards your pledge. This is the essence of progress.

So, as a board, what should you expect of your C-suite? What impact does sustainability have on their roles? What immediate actions can they take to address and align to the challenges raised by the need to support the board in the sustainability strategy and deliver on the strategic mandate?

As a powerful C-suite team, you are the ones carrying out the day-to-day implications and actions outlined above for the board. It is up to you to ensure your board gives you the mandate you need so that the business you steer will prosper and thrive over the next 5 to 10 years and beyond.

But how do you structure and delegate this into your organization? How do you align and communicate this with clarity?

Let's outline the practical consequences of the alphabet soup and the 1-2-3s in terms of C-suite roles.

Some roles are affected more than others. Each role has accountabilities for outcomes within the business that need assessment and action. Each role has stakeholders to engage and align. Flowing from this are specific areas for immediate focus and challenges to be addressed.

Your sustainability responsiveness typology (Observer, Pledger, Complier, Transformer) will influence your implementation. However, all ESG elements should be addressed to reduce risk and improve long-term value creation for your business.

Chief Executive Officer and Chief Operations Officer (CEO and COO)

Vision and integration

Assess and act	Stakeholders to engage
Business model, strategy, goals, and culture	Board, investors, stock exchange (if listed), and regulators

Ask

- Ask your board for active guidance. What is the right sustainability responsiveness profile for your long-term business horizon (over decades)?
- Who can you partner and collaborate with to speed up the process of net zero and progress toward the green world of under +1.5°C?

Act

- Address impact on business model agility, license to operate, and strategic resilience.
- Communicating and setting your culture's ability to adjust rapidly to ongoing shifts in expectations to stakeholder-based decision-making.
- Enabling your up- and downstream partners to create value so that pledges in Scope 3 as well as those in Scopes 1 and 2 show progress, then results.

Challenges to address

- Ongoing: aligning stakeholder interests over the long term to address trade-offs, setting the tone from the top for action without overwhelming stakeholders (which leads to inaction).
- Short term: ensuring a consistent understanding of sustainability, what it is, why we need to act now, and what's expected of every person in the organization.
- Short to medium term: ensuring plan and pace of transformation is appropriate to the challenge.

Chief Revenue Officer (CRO)

Growth and agility

Assess and act	Stakeholders to engage
Impact, resilience, value chain partnering downstream	Customers, employees, innovation

Ask

- What does your pledge mean to your downstream value chain?
- Where are the short-term wins that will build credibility (and ensure contracts) as RFP pressure for ESG and Scope 1, 2, and 3 transparency increases?

Act

- Align sales teams (and marketing) with tools and conversation pieces so that they can deliver compounding growth on yearly targets and implement sustainability strategy.
- Evaluate product and service/distribution/market mix for opportunities and to identify if any of the services you provide are threatened.

Challenges to address

- Ongoing: collaborating with customer value chain to deliver on pledge.
- Short term: sales targets delivered while transformation planning and preparation commence.
- Short to medium term: maintaining motivation as rewards are realigned to incorporate both value sold and sustainability.

Chief Procurement Officer

Supply chain

Assess and act	Stakeholders to engage
Impact, resilience, value chain partnering upstream	Suppliers, employees, regulators

Ask

- What does your pledge mean to your upstream value chain?
- Where are the short-term wins that will reduce risk while building credibility and ensuring data quality in ESG reporting as pressure for ESG and Scope 1, 2, and 3 transparency increases?

Act

- Align procurement teams (and finance) to pledge and plan with policies and processes so that they can deliver on yearly targets inclusive of sustainability.
- Evaluate supplier and supply chain mix for opportunities and if any of the services you provide are at threat.
- Establish supply chain ethics standards to mitigate risks.

Challenges to address

- Ongoing: collaborating with supplier value chain to deliver on pledge.
- Short term: procurement standards incorporate pledge targets for transparency while transformation planning and preparation commence.
- Short to medium term: aligning motivation through upstream value chain and internal employees with consistent values and standards so both value and sustainability are achieved.

Chief Financial Officer (CFO)

Money

Assess and act	Stakeholders to engage
Forward-leaning statements, data, and progress so that your statements have financial-world credibility (EESG key)	Finance: banks, creditors, investors, regulators

Ask

- What does your pledge mean to value creation and financial scenarios?
- Where are the short-term wins that will reduce risk while building credibility with financial markets?
- What transparency is required for stakeholders and thus data quality in ESG reporting as short- and medium-term pressure for ESG and Scope 1, 2, and 3 transparency increases?

Act

- Align finance teams and policies to pledge and plan so that internal and external investments deliver on yearly targets inclusive of sustainability (EESG).
- Evaluate finance mix for opportunities and threatened funds.
- Select and develop future sources of funds for alignment with long-term interests.

Challenges to address

- Ongoing: finance value creation addressing trade-offs between short-term results and long-term strategic sustainability to deliver on your pledge. Collaborate with internal audit so that organizational risk culture balances needs for compliance and needs for growth.
- Short term: finance standards incorporate pledge targets for transparency while transformation planning and preparation commence.
- Short to medium term: monitor, align and control (influence) interests so that corporate risk appetite and delegations include both financial and sustainability criteria.

Chief Human Resources Officer (CHRO)

People and culture

Assess and act	Stakeholders to engage
Culture: values alignment, KPIs, reviews, and renumeration. Key for internal credibility	Employees, NC, RC

Ask

- What does your pledge mean to internal culture, values, and compensation and benefits? Where are the short-term wins that will build credibility with your talent?
- What will be needed for medium- to long-term trust?
- What adjustments are needed to talent pool and succession planning to ensure your pledge is delivered on, along with ESG reporting, while recognizing Scope 1, 2, and 3 complexities?

Act

- Identify long-term culture that integrates sustainability-based decision-making to deliver strategic sustainability.
- Align compensation, benefits, KPIs, and HR policies to pledge and plan so that internal and external staff deliver on yearly targets inclusive of sustainability (EESG).
- Collaborate with internal audit and external consultants to identify culture risks for preemptive attention.

Challenges to address

- Ongoing: creating a culture that creates value for all material stakeholders while addressing trade-offs between short term results and long-term strategic sustainability to deliver on your pledge. Collaborate with internal audit so that organizational risk culture balances needs for compliance and needs for growth.
- Short term: HR standards and policies incorporate pledge targets for transparency while transformation planning and preparation commence.
- Short to medium term: monitor, align, and control (influence) interests so that culture, and corporate risk appetite, delegations, and KPIs integrate values and financial and sustainability criteria.

Chief Information officer (CIO)

Information, data, and technology

Assess and Act	Stakeholders to engage
New data, data analytics, and value-chain transparency	Employees, technology partners

Ask

- What does your pledge mean to technology, data, and security architecture?
- Where are the short-term wins that will build resilience with internal talent and technical partners? What will be needed for medium- to long-term trust so that agile action is possible?
- What adjustments are needed to IT strategy to ensure your pledge is delivered, along with ESG reporting, while recognizing Scope 1, 2, and 3 complexities?

Act

- Identify long-term IT strategy to deliver strategic sustainability.
- Align technologies, data, and policies to pledge and plan so that data, digitalization, and automation deliver on yearly targets inclusive of sustainability (EESG).
- Collaborate with internal audit and external consultants to identify technology risks for preemptive attention.

Challenges to address

- Ongoing: strive for IT readiness that creates value and pro-vides value, enabling stakeholders to navigate trade-offs between short-term results and long-term strategic sus-tainability to deliver on your pledge. Collaborate with internal audit so that IT risks are incorporated into sustainability.
- Short term: IT standards and policies incorporate pledge targets for transparency while transformation planning and preparation commence.
- Short to medium term: monitor, align, and control (influence) interests so that IT and data enable financial and sustainabil-ity criteria.

Chief Marketing Officer (CMO)

Message and substance

Assess and act	Stakeholders to engage
Internal truth and aligned values will ensure that your statements have external credibility	Community, NGOs, media

Ask

- What does your pledge mean to customers and communities?
- Where are the short-term wins that will build credibility as NGO and media pressure for substance in ESG and Scopes 1, 2, and 3 increases?

Act

- Align key messages so marketing standards are aligned to pledge, plan, and progress.
- Update crisis communications protocols for risks arising from gaps between what's said, what's done, and what's perceived as real by external stakeholders.

Challenges to address

- Ongoing: alignment of brand promise, company values, and actions to pledge.
- Short term: review all materials to ensure appropriate positioning of pledge.
- Short to medium term: maintaining respect and relationships with media as organization shifts, learns and improves in its sustainability performance.

Chief Risk Officer (CRO(2))

Risk and uncertainty

Assess and act	Stakeholders to engage
Future casting, scenarios, and value chain along with capacity of the organization (and value chain) to adapt for mid-term LTO risk and medium/long-term risks to exit value and sustainability	Board, board risk committee, insurance

Ask

- What does your pledge mean to short, medium, and long-term business scenarios?
- Where are the risks that need immediate attention as the expectation for substance in ESG and Scopes 1, 2, and 3 increases?

Act

- Evaluate and align risk profile at enterprise level.
- Update risk management protocols for risks arising from pledge, other businesses moving to transition to under +1.5°C business models, and regulatory acceleration.
- Evaluate future insurability and assess probabilities of stranded and toxic assets.

Challenges to address

- Ongoing: alignment of enterprise risk profile to forward-looking scenarios and pledge.
- Short term: review all materials to ensure appropriate positioning of pledge.
- Short to medium term: maintaining respect and relationships with media as organization shifts, learns, and improves in its sustainability performance.

Chief Transformation and Strategy Officer (CTSO)

Strategy, adaptability and capacity to endure

Assess and act	Stakeholders to engage
Integration of strategy and results delivery. To run 5 years and not deliver will expose the enterprise to significant risks.	CEO, board, sustainability committee, transformation programs

Ask

- What does your pledge mean to short, medium, and long-term options and scenarios?
- If your business does not have a pledge, plan, and progress, what strategic risks does this generate?
- Where are there untapped opportunities in what substance is expected in ESG and Scopes 1, 2, and 3?

Action:

- Evaluate and align business transformation strategies and programs at enterprise level.
- Update program management protocols for responsibilities and arising from pledge, other businesses moving to transition to under +1.5°C business models, and regulatory acceleration.
- Evaluate mid-term implications of circularity to business model.

Challenges to address

- Ongoing: alignment of strategy and transformation to forward-looking scenarios, pledge, and science-based targets.
- Short term: review short-term tactics and project portfolios to ensure they are appropriate, given your pledge.
- Short to medium term: enhance (or establish) rapid, agile change capacities to keep up with and get ahead on the pipeline of changes underway.
- Medium term: understand how circularity and shifting to a circular economy may influence strategic sustainability.

Chief Innovation Officer (CIO(2))

Innovation

Assess and act	Stakeholders to engage
Full integration of sustainability across all the types in ESG (carbon, greenhouse gas, diversity . . .)	CEO, board, employees, suppliers

Ask

- What do sustainability and your pledge mean across stakeholders?
- Where are there opportunities for product or service innovation that will generate financial and sustainability value?

Act:

- SWOT & STEEPLE analysis of current innovation pipeline to identify opportunities.
- Update innovation pipeline to incorporate sustainability-based priorities.

Challenges to address

- Ongoing: alignment of innovation, company values, and actions to your pledge.
- Short term: review all projects to ensure gaps to delivery on your pledge are identified.
- Short to medium term: encourage a culture of innovation adoption across the organization so that proven R&D/ projects can be deployed rapidly after innovation.

Head of Audit

Assurance, rigor and reliability

Assess and act	Stakeholders to engage
Robustness of assurance for forward-looking statements and for issues across the value chain	Board, audit committee, stock exchange (if listed), investors

Ask

- What do your pledge and strategy mean to value creation and forward-looking disclosures like sustainability reporting?
- Where are the short-term controls necessary to reduce risk while building capacity to deliver?
- What transparency is required for stakeholders and thus what data is reported to which locations?

Act:

- Evaluate the organization's ability to tolerate an increasingly transparent black box.
- Specify the minimum bar for compliance on a forward-looking basis so that anticipate reviews reduce medium-term risk.
- Identify the assurance support you will need for forward-looking statements made to regulators and the public.

Challenges to address

- Ongoing: long-term value creation addressing trade-offs between short-term results and long-term strategic sustainability while delivering on your pledge. Collaborate with finance and HR so that organizational risk culture balances needs for compliance with needs for growth.

- Short term: use anticipate reviews to preempt medium-term risks. Verify standards, including science-based targets selected, so that robust credible metrics inform progress and reports.
- Short to medium term: evaluate and design assurance so that conflicts of interest, corporate risk appetite, and delegations integrate financial and sustainability criteria.
- Continually: verify alignment and understanding of actions so that time is not lost.

Bottom line

- Greensight strategies involve significantly more than looking at carbon emissions and having the finances to operate as a going concern.
- Scope 3 is a gamechanger in strategic risk management.
- Legal boundaries have limited impact on responsibility.
- Ensure that your sustainability strategy addresses business model implications.
- The pace of economic cost internalization is accelerating.
- Act early.
- Pledge, set your pathway, and be ready with proof of action.
- Establish your sustainability governance now so that it beds into the business operations and culture.
- Engage all members of your leadership team and then your organization.

PART 5

THE FUTURE IS GREEN

I began my journey as a director by looking up a mountain for a way forward, trying to deal with unfunded debt while delivering to my stakeholders. My board and I did just that. The management team did just that. It was a collective effort requiring clear vision, well-delineated roles, and not a small amount of hope.

Today, on the forefront of the Sustainability Surge, the IPCC calls out hope: "We have options in all sectors to at least halve emissions by 2030."[31] Halving emissions by 2030 while minimizing our exposure to all elements of ESG and continuing to deliver on our promises to shareholders is the biggest challenge of our times.

31 IPPC Arc 6 Report, Press release April 4, 2022: https://www.ipcc.ch/2022/04/04/ipcc-ar6-wgiii-pressrelease/.

As leaders, we wield roles that involve significant legal, financial, and ethical responsibilities. We are in an enviable position, too, for we have it in our power to influence the course of history.

With this book in hand, you've got a framework to assess your sustainability responsiveness, analyze your business model's impact and exposure up and down the value chain, and make a plan that responds to the expectations of all stakeholders. You've got a sustainability governance structure that will help you and your team align on who does what, and when.

Our collective leadership will find a way forward to deliver net zero—with businesses that prosper and serve our stakeholders well. The foresight I'm calling Greensight is your path to creating a just and sustainable future for your company and our world.

It is my hope that this book inspires you to embrace your role and join me in meeting the sustainability transition head on.

ACKNOWLEDGEMENTS

This book would not exist if it were not for a confluence of people. Professor Rafael Ramirez invited me to the Oxford Futures Forum on scenarios and climate imaginaries in 2017. The discussions re-sparked my hope that business could be a force for making a positive difference, and reconnected me to my childhood in Africa at IITA and then in the Philippines at IRRI. Hundreds of scientists have worked for decades to have the science we have here. If it were not for them, I'd not be able to distill their insights for you.

I want to acknowledge my business colleagues and clients (many of whom I number among my friends). One who saw my first draft of this book in 2019, Sophia Porcelli—who has known me for decades—introduced me to Jacob Düer, who in turn lead me to Yash Mishra and Richard Hayer. Our collective conversations at the Alliance to End Plastic Waste were foundational to *Greensight* and to exploring the practical challenges executives face.

Coffee with Su-Yen Wong, Chairperson of SID, pushed me into fully rewriting this book in mid-2021 when she reminded me sustainability is about progress, not perfection. A call with Nick Johnson at EGN sparked an executive interest group on sustainability which showed me just where business really was. Guys, you confirmed that this book would be useful. A few months later, a zoom conversation with Andy Wilson lead to Ogilvy collaborating on the survey component of this book. Our differing perspectives also enriched the typology section of this book. Meanwhile, frequent coffees with Ken Hickson provided much-needed sanity breaks.

Wanting to refresh my approach, I enrolled in an intense, eight-week program at the Cambridge Institute for Sustainability Leadership. This brought present-day data to principles I'd learned way back. It was there I realized how little was written for boards and transition leadership. The Greensight spark was light.

Wider afield, the Change Leaders at the University of Oxford, served as a collective of wisdom, as a caring community, and as a rigorous sounding board. This book is better for you. Rick, Dave, Eileen, Roberto, Darine, Mike, Mariann, Dirk, Rebecca, Monika, Alex, Deborah, Cecille, Sharon, and Ute, you've each added to this. Martin Thomas, Margareta Barchan and Wessel Pretorius— without you, we'd not have created this community. Nor would I have written my first book, much less this one.

To my TLBS running buddies, Isabella, Alan, Christine, Jade, Lisa and Colleen—thank you for getting me back into writing. Matt, Lisa and Col, my practice is so much more enjoyable these days.

And friends, Andrea Edwards, Lavinia Thanapathy, Leanne Taylor, Hema Prakesh, Mark Bryant, Sonja Piontek, Kris Wadia, Louisa Lee, Jonathan Cheung, Tanvi Gautham, Raghu Murthukrishnan,

Karen Leong, Cathy Johnson, Byron Nifakis, Wendy Tan, Natalie Turner, Sue Breniman, and Karsten Warneke—your belief in me and friendship has kept me afloat these years. You remind me that sustainability is equally about people as it is the planet.

Louisa, Cheri, and Karl, you are the magic behind my books that pulls the pieces together, polishing the phrases, the graphics, and the layout. Many thanks for being on my team. And for sticking with me through the iterations.

Most of all, this book would not be possible if it wasn't for John C. Flinn and Alice J. Flinn getting on a plane with my sister and me back when I was seven, to go to Nigeria just after the Biafran war. Dad, your lived example continues to inspire me to step into the as-yet-not-created and do want visionaries do: create a better future. Mum, my thanks to you on so, so many accounts. Also step-dad Nick, my siblings Susan, Sarah, Matt, and Georgie, and my nieces and nephews—you give me a reason to create this better future.

To each and every one of you who read this, my gratitude and thanks to you for being here and seeing the possibilities that exist, even with the challenges we face. Together, we shall create this future.

ABOUT THE AUTHOR

Joanne Flinn is an award-winning business advisor and author. Joanne led the country practice for Financial Services Consulting at PricewaterhouseCoopers in Thailand, sat on the IT ExCo at DBS in Singapore, and co-founded the Change Leaders, in collaboration with Saïd Business School at the University of Oxford and HEC, Paris. Her clients include start-ups ecosystems to the Fortune 500 enterprises and $1.5 billion funds.

Twice a TEDx speaker, Joanne has keynoted on four continents at industry events including the Project Management Institute (PMI) and the Asian Banker. She is a regular contributor to the Oxford Futures Forums.

She advises boards and the C-suite on how address the twin challenges of growth and ESG, facilitates Greensight leadership workshops to help leadership teams align on their sustainability direction, and runs Winning Deep programs for teams within organizations so that they understand, gain mastery, and act on sustainability-based business transformation.

Joanne enjoys travel, seeing her family in Tasmania and, as the artist Booth Aster, upcycling textiles into sculptures.

APPENDICES

Nine board sustainability Q&As

These Q&As reflect the questions that senior executives and boards frequently ask me.

1. Is a pledge needed?

Pledges are not legally compulsory . . . yet. However, they're highly recommended. Strategically, defining your ambition through a pledge is useful for focus, both internally for alignment of your organization and externally with your stakeholders.

In some industries, like international shipping, it's a requirement to achieve specific 2030 and 2050 targets.

2. Is setting an ambition different from greenwashing?

An ambition is where you set a goal, like a net-zero pledge for 2030. You draft plans to have a road map of how to get there. Metrics help you track and progress reports demonstrate how you are doing. You share what you are learning so others can advance faster, because bringing a planet back from rusty is the opposite of a competition. And you highlight where what you have said is independently verified or assured.

Your ambition acknowledges there is a feasible way forward and announces that you are on the journey.

Greenwashing is seeing a marketing spin on something that is happening in the business and publishing it as if it's meaningful and reflects your entire operation. It's not a white lie. Greenwashing is misrepresentation. Avoid this. It's all surface.

Pop Quiz: If a business says it's green, yet 2% of its revenue come from green sources, is this greenwashing?

A) 2% does not look material.
B) While it's not material, if it's backed up with a pledge, a plan and progress, it could be ambition.
C) They acknowledge it's not material yet. It's backed up with a pledge, a plan, and progress toward a committed 2030 goal. They publicly share warts and beauty spots as they learn to help others accelerate. It's an ambition.

Greenwashing is misrepresentation in case A. Cases B and C reflect substance.

As a board, you will need to make the judgement call on whether B or C is right for you. Your industry rules, customer base, or competitive positioning may determine this.

3. Is physical materiality the same as financial materiality?

Materiality is driven by outcome.

Once you have assessment data, you will need to guide your organization to set materiality thresholds for your business.

This is about you as a board and as a C-suite setting new decision-making rules.

The test for materiality is different from that for setting financial thresholds.

Remember, in sustainability, we are looking first at impact on the physical world. How much carbon are we producing? How many acres of forest are we razing? And we are looking at the entire value chain.

The test in the 1-2-3s is to see if including or excluding an item would influence decisions or actions that affect the achievement of your ambition.

Let's make this tangible. Say a company has a reporting target of x% reduction in carbon. Leadership is in a meeting working through the inevitable trade-off choices about processes, projects, and Capex. They have three options in front of them at equivalent investment levels.

Option 1 creates a 2% impact—and the carbon target is still achieved.

Option 2 also creates a 2% impact—but in this case, the target would be missed.

Option 3 only creates a 0.1% impact in the next quarter, but over 5 years the compounding impact of the process escalates like a hockey stick into a liability.

As Option 1 would not affect the target, it's not material. Options 2 and 3 are material, as they enable your business to deliver on its disclosure targets.

This is the thinking behind the question, "Would this be seen to influence any decision or action taken by users of it?" You don't know what you don't know until you measure it.

The goal of these protocols is to ensure substantive change in the green scenario direction. While promises and pledges are the first step (covered earlier), the next stage is action.

In this respect, the GHG Protocol process is clearly designed by people who did not come down in the last shower of rain. Substance is what it's about.

Who determines materiality?

Materiality in whose eyes? Materiality is a term that is used in multiple places. Let's clarify materiality using the three questions that open this section.

> SQ1: What is are you doing to sustainability?

> SQ2: What is sustainability doing to you?

> SQ3: What are you going to do?

a. Materiality re: SQ1— *What are you doing to sustainability?* In the GHG Protocol discussion (see section: It's all about value, page 42), the word ALL was emphasized. Until you get the data on your emissions, you do not have visibility into the impact you are creating. Once you have data, then work through materiality on the basis of impact. For example, methane has 300 times the impact of carbon, so you may find that a 5% reduction per annum in methane emissions delivers significantly more results than a 20% reduction in carbon.

b. Materiality re: SQ2— *What is sustainability doing to you?* This is a value creation and enterprise risk management question for boards. It's the classic "grow but don't blow up" scenario. In this case, it's about understanding the direction of the wind that blows from your key stakeholders, the speed of change in their expectations of you (remember that climate and sustainability do not conform to the Rule of 72), and the impact and opportunities of your business model. The bottom line is a desire to understand **whether your business will last**.

This is the space of strategy and sustainability, business model and culture adequacy, risks and responses for transition risks and stranded assets. It's about the actions you as a board need to take to set direction for future relevance, to future-proof and to be future ready.

c. Materiality re: SQ3— *What are you going to do?* This is about sequencing action and priorities, decision-making, and choices on the ground. Design, plan, and manage your strategic transformation program. This is the active space of leadership and management, day-to-day.

This is where clarity, understanding, and alignment become precursors to success. Otherwise, your people will continue to act based on their own understanding or old priorities.

4. How does economics fit in with ESG?

The silent E of ESG is economics. If your business is not a going concern, then all else is irrelevant.

- E as in environment is getting the focus. To paraphrase and adapt General Eisenhower, environmental sustainability is important, but it's not urgent in the next 24 hours. He called smart organizations and leaders Quadrant 2 thinkers. They know that liability and risk reduction take time. They know that doing good, taking opportunities, and aligning to an updated purpose take time.

  Remember that Nokia and Kodak had great technology but were unable to keep catch up with new technology trends. You could say they were out-teched. By improving your sustainability responsiveness, you reduce your risk of being out E-ed.

- S or social elements often get seen as one for later. After all, if no one is screaming, is action necessary? Yet early mover Paul Polman said, in *Net Positive*, that he wishes he'd paid more attention to social elements earlier. For businesses in Australia, social factors like modern slavery, as distasteful as that sounds, are already part of the supply-chain liability faced by directors. Overall, see the social part of ESG as an AND rather than an OR. As a bonus, S elements are recognized in the Sustainable Development Goals (SDGs) as an accelerator. At the financial level: S&P reports that businesses with stronger diversity and inclusion results were less likely to be defendants in federal court cases.[32]

- G, or governance, can receive the least focus. Yet paradoxically, this is the one where you have the most influence. As a leader, you influence tone from the top, decision-making, culture, and ethics. These set the framework for rules, processes, policies, and data.

5. *Percentage or absolute?*

The GHG Protocol recommendation is to look for ratios that help guide your business in heading in the right direction. Productivity and efficiency ratios are popular as they allow a scaling business to see an n% reduction in in the intensity of impact. These are considered a starting point to be matured toward an absolute target.

Here's a business situation example:

> If your baseline is 2% emissions and producing 100 units and then you achieve a 50% reduction in emissions per unit, hurrah! Your intensity has dropped. However, if your business then scales and you now produce 1,000 units at the better emissions rate, your business now has contributed more damage overall—200 to 1,000 units. The goal is to be able to drop intensity as you scale so that your business's total emissions contribution decreases.

32 "The Sounds of Silence: No Response Speaks Volumes," S&P Global Market Intelligence, March 2022.

Any business with a scaling or unicorn ambition needs to build absolute sustainability targets into their business metrics to reduce exposure to contingent liabilities over the next decade.

Absolute targets can be supported by relative (percentage) targets at the operational and business unit levels.

6. *Design for substance*

Here are some more greenhouse gas insights for you as a board to reduce your risks.

Baselines

Your baseline says, "This is where we were on X date." It's a starting point for progress. The GHG Protocol is aware how risky it is for the planet to enable a business to increase emissions by delaying measurement.

Some organizations may delay assessing where they are now in the belief the delay will gives them a higher base in the future, from which they'll reduce. Know that delays increase your risk and the contingent liabilities on your business.

Additionality

The GHG Protocol sees the role projects, or actions, have in mitigating potential climate effects. They look for what is called additionality. In other words, if project X is not done, would results be different anyway? For example, if you don't fly but the plane still flies, has anything really changed?

Offsets

Offsets are generally not encouraged. Offsets, including green-house gas trades where used, are reported separately. While they look good on the books, in terms of net-net on the planet, carbon—or another greenhouse gas—was produced in the first place, and that's what we want to avoid. In addition, there is significant debate on the quality of offsets. Some are sold to multiple parties. Some are not likely to deliver stated benefits. Given the dubious benefit of offsets, the GHG Protocol requires reporting your actual emissions and any offsets and trades separately.

Permanence

To report a reduction in your greenhouse gas emissions, you are expected to make permanent changes. If you do something in the business to reduce emissions that is easy to reverse, either deliberately or accidently, you can report it. However, it's in a different reporting category, as the GHG Protocol wants to ensure that reductions are locked in.

Second-order effects count

Reporting includes small, unintended consequences of changes you make that have impacts on your upstream and downstream value chain. For example, if a change in your product increases the energy used by end customers, your Scope 3 emissions increase. If you reduce the amount of waste your product creates at its end of life in a customer's hands, your Scope 3 reduces.

7. What are the fundamentals of sustainability reporting?

Your sustainability reports should include the following:

- Material ESG factors for the continuity of your business
- Material risks and opportunities in the context of their value chain
- Scope 1, 2, and 3 with notes on exclusions and justifications
- Targets/ambitions with time frames
- Sustainability reporting framework (describe the standards you are using)
- Board statement on the role the board and management play in the governance of sustainability issues
- Data sources and quality, methodologies, and assumptions including principles used for forward-looking statements and allocations methods
- Optionally, include more granular insights for credibility based on the standard.

For example, the GHG Protocol recommends:

- ☐ Cumulative Scope 3 emissions from your value chain from the past
- ☐ Qualitative commentary on your data
- ☐ Sequestration, removals, and avoided emissions outside of Scopes 1, 2, and 3
- ☐ Assurance—the form this takes will depend on the issue you're reporting (for example, methane emission from a farm would have a different assurance process than carbon from a diesel truck)

- ☐ Performance indicators and intensity ratios
- ☐ Partner engagement and performance
- ☐ Benchmarks
- ☐ Bought or sold credits
- ☐ Contractual provenance of emissions risks and obligations
- ☐ Separate reporting of biogenic carbon arising from the natural carbon cycle of harvesting, digestion, fermentation, decomposition, and combustion.

Whom do you do business with?

If you do business with one of the industries below, this is a heads-up. They are part of an industry that is heavily affected by climate change, and one that is key to transitioning to a low-carbon, green-scenario economy.

In Singapore, listed companies in these industries must disclose (as in it is mandatory, it's not optional for them) climate-related risks.

All financial years commencing	Industry (as identified by TCFD)
1 January 2023	Financial
	Agricultural, food and forest products
	Energy
1 January 2024	Materials and buildings
	Transportation

Source: SGX Practice Note 7.6, (s) 4.9, Sustainability Reporting Guide, Updated 1 January 2022.

Companies you do business within these industries will ask you for your sustainability data so that they can complete their Scope 3 disclosures. If you cannot provide this data, you may soon be off their supplier lists. Being able to certify that your business complies with ethical procurement standards such as CIPS and ethical business standards will be increasingly valuable and contribute to your license to operate.

Their timelines will determine the timeline you have in which to prepare and contribute positively or negatively to your sustainability risks.

8. What are the 20 categories to consider in your value chain?

When you assess your business model, risk profiles, or report, note that even today you are expected to understand:[33]

- Past: emission that **may have** occurred over the life of the business
- Future: that **are expected** to occur in the future because your activities in the current period have long-term impact.

If you are a board member, know that delays in understanding what you are producing (past and future) in your value chain will lead to increased personal risk. As the General Counsels in Singapore put it,

---

33 Increased transparency suggests it's good practice to get insight into these now.

"It is no longer possible for any person holding a position of responsibility to claim that he or she has no knowledge of the adverse effects of climate change or what its major causes are."[34]

If the man on the street understands climate change, so can boards.

So, what should you look for? Start with the following 20 categories.[35]

Upstream

This focus on the past is about what has happened before resources make it to your entities. If a resource had a negative impact a decade ago and was stored, creating no negative impact, over the last 10 years, you still need to understand and recognize the original damage.

34 Jeffry W.T., Chan S.C., Joseph Chun, Ernest Lim, Peter Doraisamy, Queck Wen Jian (Gerald), Legal Opinion on Directors' Responsibilities and Climate Change Under Singapore Law, April 2021, p 11.
35 The categories include categories established by the GHG Protocol and additional categories highlighted by the SGX Practice Note 7.6 Sustainability Reporting Guide.

Category	Notes
1. Purchased goods and services	Cradle to gate[36]
2. Capital goods	Cradle to gate
3. Fuel/energy-related activities	That is not within Scopes 1 and 2 Cradle to gate
4. Upstream transportation and distribution	
5. Waste generated in operations	Includes solids and wastewater
6. Business travel	
7. Employee commuting	Yours, franchisees, telecommuters, contractors, and any outsourced talent
8. Upstream leased assets	Includes lifecycle emissions for manufacturing or constructing leased assets
9. Social impact on local communities	This is a polite way of asking if you are using modern slavery, disrupting community survival, or destroying cultural artifacts
10. Corruption	While this is part of corporate governance, it is also a material sustainability factor in some industries

36 Cradle to gate: from wherever in the process the impact (for example, a greenhouse gas emission) occurs. This could be from extraction from the ground to the moment the product arrives at the end buyer's doorstep and can include agricultural activities, land use, and land use changes.

Downstream

These are future-oriented. This is about understanding the consequence of the use of your products and services going forward.

Category	Notes
11. Upstream transportation and distribution	Including your customers' customers' transportation
12. Processing of sold products over their lifetime	Product includes services
13. Use of sold products	Indirect use-phase emissions and maintenance
14. End-of-life treatment of sold products	
15. Downstream leased assets	Includes life cycle emissions
16. Franchises	
17. Investments	If done with the objective of making a profit, include impact created by the investment[37]
18. Social impact on local communities	Includes health and quality of life impacts on those who use your products and services
19. Corruption	While this is part of corporate governance, it is also a material sustainability factor in some industries

37 GHG Protocol: Corporate Value Chain Scope 3, Accounting and Reporting, published 2011, p 53.

Within your entities

The 19 categories above also apply to your Scope 1 and 2 disclosures. They help you understand your own operations. There is one more. Stock exchanges are asking for transparency on this category, as it has high correlation to superior long-term performance.

Category	Notes
20. Gender, skills, and experience	Diversity enhances decision-making, risk alertness, and responsiveness to change

Source: Section 4.5 of the SGX Practice Note 7.6 Sustainability Reporting Guide.

The purpose of these 20 categories is to give you, as a board, visibility into the total expected lifetime impact of your products and your business.

If you're on a board, ensure that your risk management practices pick up these risks and responsibilities so that you can incorporate these into your sustainability strategy, ensure your sustainability reporting is at the quality you need and engage your C-suite and management to ensure ESG factors are monitored on an ongoing basis and properly managed. More on this in Sections 3, 4, and 5.

9. *What do you need to do to have substance to support your opinion in your sustainability report?*

Given the speed with which expectations are shifting on you as a listed company director, what can give you confidence, when signing off on your annual report or sustainability report, that the business is strategically sustainable? How do you ensure there is integrity between what you report to the stock exchange and investors and what is said and done in respect to other stakeholders? For example, if you've issued a statement that a product will reduce pollution, yet NGOs onsite see pollution, this damages director credibility.

If you are not a director in a listed company, you may be tempted to breathe a sigh of relief. However, as a director, you have legal duties including a duty of care to your company. You have responsibilities for situations that may be called negligence. Boards that fail to take adequate action towards sustainability may face these charges. Shareholders will be as interested in these questions as the stock market is. And as a founder, much like a parent, you'll have a vision for what the company can do. There is pressure to act in alignment with this too.

As a director of an unlisted company, you do not face stock exchange pressures for disclosure. But other providers of funds like funds managers, private equity, and banks are likely to expect of you to progressively lift your game towards listed standards.

For all businesses, regulatory change, along with customer and supplier/partner change, implies value chain impacts. Which in turn mean business models will be affected.

In no way does this overlook community and NGOs—these entities will continue to scrutinize all businesses, large and small, and hold them to account for actions taken or not.

Books, standards, and regulations

A book like this is not written alone. It's based on the work of many, many people. In business, the alphabet soup can be daunting. Here are books that I found useful. This is followed by a list of regulations and standards referred to in this book, should you be inspired to delve deeper.

Books worth reading

Doughnut Economics by Kate Raworth

The Future We Choose by Christiana Figueres and Tom Rivett-Carnac

The Good Ancestor by Roman Krznaric

Post Growth by Tim Jackson

What We Owe Each Other by Minouche Shafik

Net Positive by Paul Polman and Andrew Winston

How To Avoid A Climate Disaster by Bill Gates

Multicapital Scorecard by Martin P. Thomas and Mark W. McElroy

The Age of Fire is Over: A New Approach to the Energy Transition by Vincent Petit

Race for Sustainability: Energy, Economy, Environment and Ethics by Ken Hickson

Standards, regulators, and regulations

Some regulations and frameworks are global; others, like those from the EU, are created for a specific region and have global influence, thanks to interconnected supply chains. Other regulations are defined by national governments. While other are based on specific industries.

The ones below have been referred to in this book.

Document	Acronym
UN Sustainable Development Goals	SDG
Global Reporting Initiative	GRI
Principles of Responsible Investment	PRI
Financial Stability Board	FSB
Sustainable Accounting Standards Board	SASB
Non-Financial Reporting Directive (EU)	NFRD
Corporate Sustainability Reporting Directive (EU)	CSRD
EU Taxonomy on sustainable actions	
Taskforce for Climate-Related Financial Disclosures	TCFD
Taskforce for Nature-Related Financial Disclosure	TNFD
International Integrated Reporting Framework	<IR>
International Financial Reporting Standards Foundation	IFRS
EU Carbon Border Adjustment Mechanism	CBAM
EU New Green Deal	
Commonwealth Climate and Law Initiative	CCLI
Smith School of Enterprise and the Environment from the University of Oxford	SSEE

Greenhouse Gas Protocol	GHG Protocol
Greenhouse Gas Protocol - Project Reporting Standard	GHG PRS
Carbon Disclosure Project	CDP
UN Global Compact	
IPCC 6th Assessment Report: Climate Change 2022: Impacts Adaption and Vulnerability	ARC6-IAV
IPCC 6th Assessment Report: Climate Change 2022: Mitigation of Climate Change	ARC6-MCC
ARC 6 Synthesis Report 2022	ARC6-SR
Sciences Based Targets Initiative	SBTi
EU Mandatory Human Rights and Environment Due Diligence Framework	mHREDD
U.S. Securities and Exchange Commission	SEC
Bursa Malaysia, the Malaysian Stock Exchange	
Singapore Stock Exchange	SGX
Bank of International Settlements	BIS
Monetary Authority of Singapore	MAS
European Banking Authority	EBA
Company House, UK	
Accounting and Corporate Regulatory Authority, Singapore	ACRA
Australia Securities and Investment Commission	ASIC
Corporate Code of Governance, Singapore	
Singapore Institute of Directors	SID
Australian Competition and Consumer Commission	ACCC